Alone.
Together.
Loved.
Forever.

# Alone. Together. Loved. Forever.

A Memoir

Ingrid Lomas

First edition 2021



The Author has made every effort to trace and acknowledge sources/resources/individuals. In the event that any images/information have been incorrectly attributed or credited, the Author will be pleased to rectify these omissions at the earliest opportunity.

This book is a memoir. It reflects the author's present recollections of experiences over time. Some names and characteristics have been changed, some events have been compressed, and some dialogue has been recreated.

This book is not intended as a substitute for the medical advice of physicians. The reader should regularly consult a physician in matters relating to his/her health and particularly with respect to any symptoms that may require diagnosis or medical attention.

ISBN 978-1-928497-00-4

Published by Ingrid Lomas using Reach Publishers' services
P O Box 1384, Wandsbeck, South Africa, 3631

Edited by Bronwen Bickerton for Reach Publishers
Cover designed by Reach Publishers
Image stock by Tatiana Syrikova from Pexels
Website: www.reachpublishers.org
E-mail: reach@reachpublish.co.za

**Ingrid Lomas**

www.ingridlomas.com

hi@ingridlomas.com

# Dedication

FOR BUDDY

My dearest little dog and companion who lovingly lay at my feet while I wrote every word of my book – and who dutifully wagged his tail in appreciation whenever I read him extracts from the book.

You have left Planet Earth but you will continue to live in my heart forever.

# Table of Contents

*The teacher learns the lessons*
*the pupil learns to teach.*

**Ingrid Lomas, 2021**

# Part 1

# The Beginning

# Chapter 1

# New Life on Planet Earth

It had been so comfortable in there for so long. Until the early hours of the 2nd January in fact. Well no, to be more precise, I started feeling a desire to escape late on New Year's Day when she started adding copious amounts of alcohol to her regular intake of cigarettes. I'd got used to the smoking and had actually become a bit of an addict myself by that stage, but the alcohol was just too much. I had no intention of becoming an alcoholic. I didn't even like the taste of the stuff, let alone the fuzzy head it left me with the next day. Before I could even make a move to identify the exit, however, she was at it again.

This time she taste-tested all the food on offer at the party but finally settled on a large helping of an ultra-spicy lamb curry, rice, sambals and garlic-saturated naan bread to add extra calories to both our waists. That was the second to last straw, the final being the chasing down of it all with a big glass of Cabernet.

Positively choking on the overkill combo of rich flavours I began frantically swimming this way and that in search of the escape route. Just when I thought I'd located it, however, down came another big gulp of Cab to put me totally off my stroke. She wasn't a regular drinker, thank God, and was of course entitled to celebrate New Year in whatever way floated her boat but that didn't automatically mean I wanted to join in. Just the opposite in fact. My desire to get out had actually turned into an urgent imperative as my arms flayed about in all directions and my feet took on a life of their own, kicking violently at the walls that encircled me.

Why, I wondered, was it proving so difficult to get on with this life? The only advantage, as far as I could tell, to still being in my mother's womb was that it enabled me to remember and reflect on the reason I was embarking on another mission to Planet Earth. I knew only too well that as soon as I arrived in the world, I'd lose all memory of what I was hoping to achieve this time round. When that time came I would have to totally rely on my inner spirit to guide me. Yet as of that moment I knew exactly what I was about.

I was an eternal spirit who had vowed to take on a human form once more to learn lessons that would further increase my vibration and get me ever closer to the values of my Maker. I believe we keep on returning until our vibration, and our connection with our Maker of whom we are part, is so strong there is no need to return. And Planet Earth is perfect for the purpose of growth. It's where negativity abounds so it offers a wonderful opportunity to increase our vibration by transforming negativity into positivity.

In fact, it's that very transformation that allows all eternal spirits to not only experience the eternally beautiful life in the hereafter, but on Planet Earth too.

Just thinking about it gave me goose bumps. I knew that provided I could stick to the game plan by learning all the lessons I wished to be exposed to, I was in for an amazing experience during my forthcoming life.

I was, however, still kicking around in my mother's womb at that precise moment in time and still wondering when I was ever going to get this mission underway. Fortunately for me my mother must have felt my frustration and displeasure as she suddenly got up and thank goodness she did. It was that sudden movement that turned me on my head, giving me an uninterrupted view down a long tunnel to freedom. Or so I hastily thought. After all I had heard her say, on many occasions over the past few months, that the grass isn't always greener on the other side – and to be honest I couldn't see much light at the end of my newly discovered tunnel or any grass for that matter. But I could hear voices.

'Bill hurry, she's coming, I just know she is.' My mother Shirley's anxious voice propelled my father Bill to impart some comforting words.

'Don't worry darling, the car's right outside ready and waiting to take you to the nursing home, but please, stop referring to my son as a she.' He laughed. Ah, good man, level-headed and prepared for all eventualities by the sound of him. It gave one pause for thought though. It seemed he was expecting a boy? Well, let's just say that he was in for a pleasant little surprise shall we? It was my turn to laugh, but of course nobody could hear me.

The next thing I sensed was that we must've all been seated in the car because what little light I'd seen previously at tunnel's end suddenly disappeared completely along with their voices. I felt seriously cut off until some external activity sent a few ripples through the bath of water in which I was reclining. It was no doubt the motion of the car starting up for its journey to the nursing home. Needless to say my escape plans were on hold yet again, but at least my mother had stopped eating and drinking.

* * *

'Oh my God, what did I do to deserve this? The pain … the pain is unbearable. Help me. Help me. Somebody please help me. Get this baby out of me.'

Shirley hadn't stopped screaming from the moment we arrived at the nursing home and quite frankly I had great sympathy for her. She didn't want me out more than I wanted to get the *hell* out.

Apparently though, and this I gleaned through my father's hushed conversation with the nurses, the gynae was also attending a New Year's Day into night party and was no doubt reluctant to rush away to deliver me. Fortunately my hearing was excellent. The loudest sounds I'd previously been subjected to, apart from the dreadful music at the party, were those of my mother practicing her opera scales, all pleasantly filtered.

Not even the midwife, it seemed, was keen on helping out in the delivery department. I by contrast was never more ready to make an appearance – yet every time I made a move to ease myself down the tunnel, where the light appeared brighter than ever before, the bloody midwife made Shirley inhale to draw me back in. It was the stuff horror stories are made of. It was also extremely physically painful for me, and by her screams, equally painful for Shirley. Actually, the word painful doesn't even describe it. Excruciating is a far better word. Plus, and this was becoming the most difficult thing for me, I was finding it hard to breathe. With every dive forward towards the light of life on Planet Earth, followed immediately after by the retraction forced on Shirley by the midwife, my air supply became more compromised.

'When is all this going to end?' Shirley screamed. *Ditto*, I screamed internally. I was pretty sure that if I didn't get out of there pretty soon, I wasn't going to make it out at all.

'I'd never … never ever have risked getting pregnant if … if I'd known the pain and … and the stress this baby was going to cause me. I don't want it anymore. Do you hear me? Just take the bloody thing away.'

I was almost shocked right out of the skin covering my newly-formed body. I mean, well, let's be frank here, what Shirley had said was totally unbelievable. Surely, as an eternal being herself, she knew all the work I'd put into planning my return? First and foremost there are all the commitments every eternal spirit has to make to themselves regarding what needs to be achieved during a new lifetime on Planet Earth.

Then we have to go about entering the ether of the planet in search of a female host who will match our individual vibration, otherwise described as our level of innate knowledge and spiritual awareness, perfectly, in order to give birth to us. No mean feat that, I can tell you. The search is extensive and thorough. After all, as each of us returns at a different vibrational level, it's imperative that we identically match the vibration of our host mother. There cannot be even the slightest margin of difference between our vibrations in order to ensure birth.

When my exhaustive search identified Shirley as the best candidate for my requirements, I obviously had no hesitation in choosing her. When I heard her saying, however, that she no longer wanted me and telling the nurses to get rid of me, or words to that affect, I couldn't help thinking I'd miscalculated somewhere along the line.

Things were definitely not going according to plan. My experiences with her difficult nature were only supposed to start *after* my birth, and they weren't supposed to be quite as difficult as they were already sounding. It's not surprising then that I began entertaining the thought that perhaps I must have made the wrong choice after all. *Maybe*, I mused, *the easiest solution for both Shirley and me will be my physical demise*. Even though it was a very low vibrational thought, I had to reluctantly acknowledge that it was *my* thought and that I had to take responsibility for it. So it was precisely what I started to pray for more than anything else.

But somehow that didn't plan out either.

'Don't worry Shirley, doctor's arrived ... it won't be long now.' The nurse seemed incredibly relieved to relay this news to my mother but Shirl wasn't buying it. 'It's all very well for you to talk nurse, you're just watching all this... get it out of me ... get it out. Now. Now.' My mother's voice sounded hysterical.

'Push. Push. Push Shirley. I can see the head, baby's going to come out nicely. One more push.' Finally. The gynae had arrived. He sounded totally relaxed, no doubt as a result of his New Years' revelling. His presence might have reassured my mother but it did nothing for me.

So, before my previous wish could be granted, I was unwillingly propelled out of Shirley, not very nicely at all. In fact at such an unexpected surge of speed that it resulted in not only incredible pain for her but a prolapsed womb as well. I, of course, didn't come off that lightly either. Considering the pain and discomfort my sudden and rapid ejection had caused me, I was amazed to hear the welcoming party in the delivery room confirming that I had arrived in one piece. From a personal point of view, however, things were not that great. I was, in fact, deeply disappointed to discover that having travelled through the long dark tunnel of potential physical death into the early light of a Planet Earth morning, the air wasn't that plentiful there either.

*Golly days*, I thought, as my deprived lung capacity fully revealed itself, *surely things can only get better than this?*

It was about then that they all suddenly changed their tune about my condition.

'Blue baby. Yes blue. Blue. Oxygen nurse. Oxygen. Move. Quick. Now.' These words, bandied about by various men and women in white, were accompanied by much scurrying to and fro.

Well, that answered that concern of mine, didn't it?

'No. It's asthma. She's experiencing her first asthma attack,' declared the gynae. He sounded relieved. I can't say I was. 'Never mind Shirley, she's going to be just fine. And once I've stitched you up, so are you – good as new.'

Shirley, however, had gone very quiet, apparently with the aid of some soothing substance they'd given her. I wouldn't have minded some of it either to calm *me* down. I was already missing my daily intake of nicotine so I definitely needed something to get me over *my* trauma too. Instead of either of the aforementioned, however, I was given the oxygen they were all falling over themselves to hook me up with. It was also my first inkling that, due to my last-minute desire to terminate my birth combined with the stop start nature of my delivery, I was destined to be someone who wouldn't be able to breathe in life properly for many moons to come.

# Chapter 2

# Parents with the Right Vibes

The oxygen I was given shortly after my birth seemed to do the trick. I soon started breathing with little effort and drifted off into a pleasant little sleep. When I woke up, however, some big changes in my so far short life had taken place. Shirley, according to the nurses' chatter, was in theatre getting stitched up and I was on formula milk to stop me crying out in hunger. The formula was soya-based and decidedly tasteless compared to what I'd become used to, but beggars can't be choosers, another saying I'd heard Shirley voice from time to time. And as I hadn't exactly been presented with a menu from which to select my first meal in the world, I quickly realised I was going to have to make a choice between the formula … and the formula.

What's more, it soon became apparent that having decided against breast feeding, Shirley was in no mood to kiss and cuddle me following her surgery. To my surprise I was quickly dispatched into the loving care of my grandmother while Shirl stayed on to make a full recovery at the nursing home. My father was around, of course, but in a remote sort of way. I could see him peering at me but mostly from a distance and almost always with a focus on my head and hair. I knew he'd wanted a son. Well, he'd said so, hadn't he, just before we left for the nursing home … but surely he'd seen a baby girl before? As it turned out he was more upset about the *colour* of my hair than my sex. 'Where does this black curly hair come from Maysie?' I heard him ask my grandmother. 'It's definitely not from my side of the family.'

I'd noticed the same thing, of course. I'd looked closely at both of them to see who I most resembled. Certainly it was not Bill, with his head of ultra-fine fair hair, nor Shirley, with her lustrous rich auburn. Could there have been a mistake of some kind? Was it at all possible that there'd been a massive cosmic error? Had I erroneously been born to the wrong parents? It was such a terrifying thought in fact that I decided it was one that would be best ignored.

* * *

Bill continued to look worried until one wonderful day when his suspicious frown was suddenly replaced by a delighted grin. I was baffled at his sudden turnabout, until he held me up to the mirror and I caught sight of my new hair. Blonde bum-fluff. I had no idea until that very moment that my black curls had only been temporary. Not just that, but my mother's calorie-rich diet, generously shared with me, seemed to have also fallen away at the same time, revealing my large blue eyes. Two identical faces gazed back at me. Oh well, no mistake there, Bill was definitely my father – but was Shirley really my mother? Just joking of course. Come what may I knew from that moment on that Shirley, Bill and I were destined to be together – even if Shirley had reservations.

'Isn't life unfair?' she said, a refrain I was to hear throughout her life. 'She's an engaging little soul and her colouring is good … but … well honestly, why did she have to inherit the texture of your hair when she could have had mine?'

'Relax darling, her hair and eyes suit her beautifully,' Bill said modestly and chuckled. 'So glad she decided to ditch the black curls. I can only think they must have had something to do with that curry you ate.' He laughed louder this time and Shirley joined in. *I* had actually rather liked my black curls.

There was no doubt about it. In Shirley's opinion I'd come close, but I definitely hadn't ticked all the boxes at birth. With hindsight, I wonder why my perfectionist mother hadn't returned me to the nursing home and swapped me for a baby with better quality hair and more functional lungs. Or requested a refund, perhaps, at least, as some compensation for all the pain she'd experienced during my birth and which ultimately resulted in me being an only child.

'No. Definitely not. I've never considered having another child.' Shirley always declared this to all who ever asked and even on occasion to some who didn't ask. 'Ingrid positively tore me to shreds you know. Who in their right mind would consider putting themselves through that again if they knew what was in store for them?'

Yet, all that being said I had chosen Shirley to be my mother, and by association, I'd chosen Bill to be my father. So the three of us had a whole lifetime ahead of us to work through our relationship and avail ourselves of the lessons we had all chosen to learn from one another.

* * *

Talking of choosing parents, those who have good relationships with theirs will find it easier to agree to having had a hand in choosing them. Those who don't will no doubt be shaking their heads in disbelief and wondering what the *hell* I'm talking about.

*Why would I have chosen them*, you're probably saying to yourself. *If I was the one who got to choose, how come I didn't choose parents I'd get on with?*

Well that's exactly the point. In order to be ensured of our birth, we're required to choose a mother who is a perfect "vibrational" match with us. Once we get our heads around that we suddenly understand that our relationship with our parents has nothing to do with personalities and character traits. It also has nothing to do with whether they have the same interests as us, or are fun to be around, or love the way we talk, think or act – just as it was in the case of Shirley, Bill and me.

We also come to understand that we remain at the vibrational level of our parents until we choose to advance our vibrations and move on to greater heights. This doesn't necessarily mean moving away from them. On the contrary, the more evolved our vibration becomes, the more understanding and loving of our parents we can become. They are after all just like all the "teachers" we draw into our lives via matching vibrations.

We may like or dislike what they impart in varying degrees of intensity. We may love them, tolerate them, or want to get away from them as soon as we can. Nothing, however, that parents and other teachers impart is ever wasted. It can either assist us in increasing our vibration, or not, or assist us in maintaining our vibration, or not. But it's super cool to know that it's entirely up to *us* to determine what kind of life we want to live on Planet Earth and at what vibration we want to live it. It's equally cool to know that every happy or unhappy incident is a mirror image of what we are experiencing within ourselves at any given moment via the vibrations that we emit. Low vibrations attract the not so good happenings while high vibrations are responsible for the good ones. Provided we remember to act on that knowledge, we can choose to always be on a high. Or not.

# Chapter 3

# Learning to Play My Part

I must admit that it seemed like a foreign place from the word go. I'm referring, in case you're wondering, to my family home. The one I shared with my parents.

I know I considered being sent to live with my grandmother while Shirley stayed on at the nursing home to recover from my birth as more than a little strange and unsettling at the time. Yet as it turned out, leaving the secure environment of my grandmother's "happy house" to go "home" with Bill and Shirley proved to be a far more disturbing experience.

All three of us, Bill, Shirley and I, lived with my grandparents for a while following Shirley's return from the nursing home, during a period when the finishing touches were being made to *our* home. So when the day arrived and we had to go and live in it I should have been far more ready for our departure than I was. Yet I suppose no matter how often I heard snippets of conversation relating to where we would be moving in due course, nothing could truly have prepared me for leaving. I had after all formed such a strong bond with my grandmother that the thought of not seeing her every single day, as I'd got used to doing, was deeply traumatic.

The home I'd shared with my grandparents seemed perfect in every way. It was always warm and sunny and filled with a constant stream of happy, laughing people. No wonder it was affectionately referred to as May's Club House.

*'Surprise, surprise, it's me again Maysie dear, your almost daily visitor. I suddenly found myself in the neighbourhood and wondered if you'd mind if I just popped in to say hello?'*

*'Eleanor, how wonderful that you did. A day without you would be awful,'* Nana laughed. *'And your timing is perfect, we were just about to have tea. Come in, come in.'*

*'What must you think Maysie. I've just realised it's lunch time so this is positively the worst time of the day to arrive on your doorstep unannounced?'*

*'Jill, how lovely to see you dear – come in and join us, we've only just started eating and there's plenty to go round.'*

*'Oh Maysie are you sure? It's just that Peter and the kids are also here, they're in the car … so …?'*

*'Well that's wonderful, naturally you're all welcome – besides I'd love to see Peter and the children again – it's been ages.'*

*'Dearest May, please forgive me for arriving empty-handed again. I was going to bake a cake and bring it over but honestly my baking skills are so bad … I decided against it. I think I'm going to have to take lessons – I mean your cakes are always sooo delicious that one from me would quite frankly be an embarrassment.'*

*'Don't be silly Fee, I'm always thrilled to see you – I don't need to see a cake as well. In any event we seem to have over baked today so the last thing we need is yet another cake.'*

The irresistibly delicious smells that constantly permeated my grandmother's house never failed to reassure me that I was living in exactly the right place. It seemed like a never-ending array of bread, cakes and biscuits accompanied by their tantalizing aromas were continually being whipped up in the kitchen – no doubt in preparation for the next bunch of hungry callers. What's more these visitors not only came to see my grandparents but to see *me* as well and they seemed to love interacting with me as much as I loved being with them.

*'Oh May, she's such an adorable little thing, so responsive, I think I'll come back again in the dead of night and steal her.'*

*'You'll probably have to join the queue in the passage if you do,'* my proud Nana laughingly replied.

There was also the wonderful smell of lavender polish liberally and lovingly applied by dear Joseph, my Nana's treasured houseman and general factotum, to ensure that there was an ever-present sheen on the floors and furniture. Then there was the constant, ever enticing, and unmistakable scent of my grandmother herself. Her wonderful perfume reassuringly lingered in every room. So much so that I always had the feeling she was close even when she wasn't.

The home I shared with Bill and Shirley didn't seem, by contrast, quite like home at all. Even though, architecturally speaking, it faced the right way, it nevertheless seemed to be somewhat lacking in light and warmth. This probably went some way to explaining the shortage of visitors by comparison with my Nana's house. But what was even more disturbing was its resemblance to a film set on struts. Efficiently painted, yet flat and uninviting on the outside, it also had a feeling of not being quite real on the inside. Its only redeeming feature, from my perspective, was the garden, to which I escaped whenever I could. It was full of pretty, sweet-smelling flowers and whenever I was allowed to, I took my dolls out there to have tea parties with them under the trees. *'Who wants to be Shirley today?'* I never failed to ask my dolls before we started our tea parties, but my question was constantly met with unresponsive, bland stares so I always ended up playing Shirley and they played themselves.

It was, however, from the *inside* of "the set" that I was able to observe my parents acting out their respective roles on a daily basis.

They were "older" parents who had married later than average back in the day and obviously had me even later. It's pretty clear that they were in no hurry to have children. In fact it's my belief that if the form of contraception they practiced at the time, known as the "Rhythm Method", hadn't let them down, it's extremely doubtful they would have had children at all.

*'Ingrid wasn't planned of course. It came as a total shock to me to find out that I was pregnant but that's the way life is I suppose.'* This interesting snippet of information divulged by Shirley was no secret, she shared it with all and sundry, so it obviously reached my ears as well and left me in no doubt that I was a mistake that simply had to be lived with.

Bill was quite a bit older than Shirley but despite the age gap he always seemed to look much younger than his years. Due to maintaining his looks with the help of exceptionally good health, by contrast with the problems Shirley experienced with hers over time, he even managed to outlive her by a year. As well as develop a "close" relationship with his caregiver in the aftermath of Shirley's passing – although it was never confirmed just how close.

They were a good-looking couple in their day, in fact Shirley was very beautiful, even though she never thought so and spent most of her life trying to improve on her appearance. They both had their share of admirers of course. He openly enjoyed female company but was unable to control his jealous streak whenever he suspected Shirley was receiving more than necessary attention from members of the opposite sex. He was, however, a caring and indulgent husband who also filled the role of father figure for Shirley who had lost her real father at a young age. Although she constantly resisted his somewhat domineering attitude towards her, she never failed to seek his opinion, which she valued, even if she didn't always act on it.

*'For God's sake Shirl, you've had all damn day to comb your hair. In case you haven't noticed, "your husband" is now home.'* Bill was leaning against their bedroom door, his suit jacket draped over his shoulder with the help

of one hand while the fingers of the other removed a cigarette from his lips. Shirley, however, continued, regardless of his comments, to attended to her hair while seated in front of her dressing table mirror.

*'Would it be too much for you to come and sit down in the lounge with me and perhaps offer me a cup of tea or even ask me how my day has been?'*

A highly irritated Shirley now looked up and surveyed him in the mirror.

*'Oh don't be so silly Bill, I'm … I'm coming through right now – it's not my fault you're home early today. I wasn't expecting you for another hour or more.'*

Bill nodded his agreement. *'Hmmm, I am early today, thought I might surprise you. I often wonder what you do here all day besides your hair and make-up. Maybe you're now involved in a redo of everything after a surprise visit from somebody else?'*

Shirley stopped applying the lipstick she was now holding to her mouth and turned away from the mirror to look at him in disgust.

*'Now you are being utterly ridiculous. I'm not sure I want to sit down and talk to you when you're in one of your stupid, and totally baseless, jealous moods.'*

They played their roles to perfection as they waited for me to play my part – while regretfully eliminating, at the same time, any talents that I didn't possess and could not, as a result, demonstrate.

* * *

*'Hello darling,'* Bill greeted Shirley with an affectionate little hug and a peck on her proffered cheek. He'd just come home from work, and now, on entering the lounge, took off his jacket and loosened his tie before collapsing into the nearest chair. *'How was your day?'* Shirley sighed and drew deeply on her cigarette as she shook her head. *'Disappointing in the extreme. Ingrid takes after you in more ways than I could possibly have imagined.'* She looked out the window in a sad sort of way before sitting down on a chair opposite him.

Bill looked resigned. *'How nice to see you too darling. And by the tone of your voice I can only assume what you've just said isn't a compliment? By the way I had a very pleasant day. Thank you for asking.'*

Disregarding his sarcasm and obvious annoyance, Shirley continued where she'd left off. *'I've almost decided to give up trying to teach her the piano – like you she appears to be tone deaf. And I might just as well stop her singing lessons as well. Apart from having difficulty singing in tune she shows no interest whatsoever in the lovely little songs I'm teaching her to help her develop an ear for music. Isn't life strange. I can't understand her disinterest; I loved my singing lessons as a child.'*

Shirley by sharp contrast with me was doubly blessed with musical ability. It had been identified early on in her life by her music teacher at the convent she attended that she had an exceptionally beautiful Soprano voice. A voice destined, with the right training, for a great future. But her talents didn't end there. It also emerged that she was a gifted classical pianist in the making and made her debut in her first concert while still at school. According to my proud Nana, Shirley could have had an outstanding career in either field.

Yet as so often happened in her day she eventually gave up on her musical aspirations and settled instead for marital bliss with Bill.

I was lying on the carpet with one ear on their largely unhappy conversation while applying what little talent I had to my colouring -in book.

*'Tell me, Ingy,'* said Bill, a note of concern in his voice, *'are you enjoying your singing lessons with Mummy?'*

*'No,'* I answered without hesitation and without looking up.

*'Oh my, why's that?'* His concern seemed to deepen.

I looked up at that point. *'I'm just … I'm just tired of … songing the same sings … every day.'*

Bill and Shirley presumably thought it was the funniest thing they'd ever heard as they both burst into gales of laughter. I, of course, assumed they were laughing at me and didn't like it at all – in fact I started to cry.

*'No, don't cry darling.'* Bill tried to placate me with his words. *'Although you probably don't realise it, what you said was very funny. Mummy and Daddy were laughing at what you said not at you. We didn't mean to hurt your feelings. Come and sit here next to me and tell Daddy what you'd prefer to singing lessons.'*

As I got up to make my way across the room to where Bill was sitting, I suddenly stopped and contemplated his question before thoughtfully answering.

*'I ... I would prefer ... to be happy.'*

Both Bill and Shirley looked perturbed as they exchanged glances.

* * *

Not surprisingly I wasn't quite sure how to perform my part in the very beginning but, after receiving some coaching in this department, I was left in no doubt as to the true nature of the role expected of me. It was that of an ever polite, tidy, well-mannered and perfectly groomed little girl who should, for the most part, be seen but not heard. A child who was also required to diligently apply herself to all her allotted tasks in order to grow up to be, and to do, all the things in life that would make Bill and Shirley happy. But not necessarily herself.

My notion of being happy at that time of my life lay fairly and squarely with being with my grandmother – so my initial reaction on arrival at this unfamiliar place called home was to cry for her day and night. This was of course much to the surprise of my parents. And of deep concern to Bill. When that didn't result in me being returned to her, I started to withdraw into myself and as a result, from the world.

*'I am very fond of Maysie as you well know Shirley, but why Ingrid constantly demonstrates a preference to being with her, rather than with us, is ... well it's worrying. Maybe you just didn't spend enough time with her when she was a*

*baby, making your mother's presence more important in her life?'*

Shirley was furious at the suggestion. *'What nonsense you talk Bill. Everyone loves my mother. Not least of all me – to suggest she has somehow managed to establish a more important role than me in my daughter's life is not only rude but ridiculous.'*

*'I said that maybe you allowed it to happen because …'*

Shirley interrupted him. *'May is a very special person who everyone wants to be with. Added to that it's quite normal for children to love being with their grandmothers when they're young. Caring grandmothers simply indulge them more. And of course that's very appealing to little children.'*

*'Yes,'* said Bill a little wearily, *'you have described Maysie's caring role in Ingrid's life more than once but …'*

Shirley ignored him. *'And that's why I keep telling you that we should encourage Ingrid to spend more time with her at this stage of her life. Although I can't bear to even think about it, my mother isn't going to be around forever … so why not let them spend time together while they can?'*

Bill nodded in a resigned sort of way.

*'Ingrid will eventually grow out of the all-consuming adoration she currently demonstrates for her. And naturally, over time, will want to be with us just as much ... In the meanwhile her spending more time with May will not only be beneficial to both of them, it will also free me up to have a bit more time for myself.'*

*'You mean more time to comb your hair don't you?'*

Bill's response, although delivered with a good-natured grin, made it's intended or unintended mark.

*'Oh very funny Bill, you're a laugh a minute. But I must warn you that your repertoire is becoming decidedly stale. If you really want to give up your day job to make more of your obvious desire to be a stand-up comedian maybe you should look at targeting more than one person.'*

* * *

The more I initially demanded my need to see my grandmother the less often, it seemed, I was permitted to do so. Oh but when I did, it was as if by magic that time appeared to stand still and joy and happiness flowed back into my world.

*'Nana, Nana,'* I exclaimed one day during a phone call I was encouraged to make to her regarding plans for the forthcoming school holidays, *'did they tell you I'm going to spend the "whole" holiday with you?'*

*'Yes my dearest, I have been told and Nana's just as excited as you are – we'll have a wonderful time together.'*

Unfortunately, *entire* school holidays spent with my grandmother became less frequent as time went by. Bill decided that Shirley and I should do more together during the holidays but no matter what we did, outings just weren't that rewarding if they didn't involve my Nana.

It was no surprise then that the withdrawn demeanour I had started to demonstrate at, and from, my parent's home eventually became the norm and permeated every facet of my life. I found that unlike my early baby years when everything in life always appeared sunny, rosy and filled with loving souls, I was now not only deeply unhappy with myself but no longer able to relate that well to other people either. Be they adults or children. In fact, the less I saw of my dearest Nana the more I began to feel that I had never really belonged on this planet in the first place. I wondered if I was, in fact, just visiting a particularly unwelcoming world. On reflection it must have been about then that my previously strong "baby" connection with my inner spirit seemed to close down completely.

*'No,'* I shook my head, *'I … I don't want to go to Sheryl's house to play. I want to stay at home and play with my own toys.'*

My feeling of not belonging was particularly evident in large gatherings when everyone else appeared to be having such a "good time". I on the other hand always seemed removed from whatever was going on. In a strange sort of "out of body" way I experienced the sensation of looking down on events rather than being involved in them. I often wondered if I experienced them in that way to try and get a clearer view of activities so that I could learn how to be a better participant. It wasn't that I considered myself superior from this lofty viewpoint. It was in fact just the opposite. I longed to be on an equal footing with everyone else so that I could immerse myself in their apparent joy and merriment, but somehow I just didn't seem to be able to connect in the way I hoped. More often than not I just gave up trying.

*'Ingrid, I hate to tell you, my love, but this is a "children's party" so why don't you just go outside and play with the others on the lawn instead of hanging around in here with all us mothers? Surely you agree Shirley?'*

*'Oh Marge, I am sorry. It would seem that I've spawned a total recluse.'* Shirley was in party mode and laughed uproariously at this observation. *'What can I say, she obviously takes more after Bill than me.'*

Most of the time, and by contrast with my feeble external attempts to integrate with others, I had an unwanted yet urgent internal desire to escape – to float away to a place where I could really feel I belonged, far from the noise and false frivolity I often witnessed from my removed perspective.

It didn't matter whether it was playtime at nursery school or parties in my early teens and everything between, the same separateness continued to prevail and the larger the gathering the more acute the feeling of not *really* belonging became. As I grew older, however, I was eventually able to master the art of *appearing* to be enjoying myself at social events. In fact I became so adept at it that nobody could possibly have guessed that I was just *pretending* to be part of the festivities – even on occasion the life and soul of the party – when in actual fact I was simply doing a good job at covering up my innermost feelings of not being part of the event.

But I had to learn the benefits of getting to that point the hard way.

* * *

'Where's my mummy? Where did she go?' Shirley had been at my side one moment but to my alarm had just seemed to disappear into thin air the very next. The feeling of abandonment this invoked in me made it difficult to prevent the tears pricking at the back of my eyes from escaping in full force.

'She's gone shopping. She'll be back to collect you later. Now don't be such a cry baby. Go outside, as you've been told, and play with the others, like all good children do at this nursery school.' These were the unwelcome words of a woman I'd never seen before. It was a different lady who'd taken me and Shirley out to the playground earlier, on this my first day. This new woman however, was the first person I encountered on my return to the reception area in search of Shirley.

Even as I enquired of her whereabouts the same thought kept going through my head. *Why*, I wondered, *has my mother just gone away like that without saying she was going?* When I asked Shirley about it, many years later, she replied, at first, that she couldn't remember the incident. Yet when I continued to press her on the matter her amnesia seemed to lift. 'Oh that … yes, yes … I do remember something … vaguely … it was such a long time ago … I think I must've taken the opportunity of leaving when you were distracted with something else, but only so as not to upset you Ingrid – for no other reason.' I, however, believe, with hindsight of course, that the decision had been made so as not to upset herself. After all she must have realised that disappearing without a word would absolve her from having to deal with any adverse reaction from me, should she have announced that she was leaving me with strangers.

'I don't want to go … and … and play outside. I want to go home and play with my dolls.' I bravely stood my ground in the nursery school's reception, despite uttering my response with a quivering lower lip.

'Now listen to me young lady, I'm not going to repeat myself. Go outside and play before I become very angry with you.'

I didn't like the nursery school and I certainly didn't warm to this stranger's harsh words either. She also frightened me, so against my better judgement I went back outside. The other children were still running around in circles banging into one another, laughing, screaming and shouting. There were so many and I really didn't want to play with any of them … their games looked very silly to me and not nice … but most of all they looked very scary. Fortunately, or so I thought, I spotted a Wendy house next to the playground and decided to go and wait in it for Shirley to return and take me home, even though I didn't have any idea when that would be.

I remember, as if it were yesterday, how dejected I felt as I opened the door but how very pleasantly surprised I'd been by what awaited me inside. A whole wall filled with shelf upon shelf of dolls appeared to be lined up for me to play with. There were so many to choose from that it took me a good while to make my selection. I eventually chose one who reminded me of my favourite doll at home and I began talking to her. 'You've got a ribbon in your hair that makes you look just like … like my bestest doll, Angel. So I'm going to call you Angel too.' I began to happily coo over Angel the second, as I rocked her in my arms. Suddenly and quite unexpectedly, another little girl ran into the Wendy house. She looked at me with distaste and then proceeded to pull Angel away from me.

'My doll,' the little girl screamed. 'No, no. You're naughty. She's my *dollie*, you can't have her.' I retaliated by attempting to grab Angel back. At that precise moment the nasty lady who'd ordered me to go outside and play with the other scary children entered the Wendy house. This was no doubt in response to all the noise we were making. 'Give that doll back to the nice little girl immediately,' she commanded. At first I thought she was speaking to the intruder who had snatched Angel from my arms. It soon became apparent, however, that she was ordering *me* to let go of *my doll* so that *the would be thief* could have her. I couldn't quite believe what was happening but I'll never forget how terribly upset I was by this very unhappy incident and how I cried uncontrollably at the injustice of it all.

I now realise of course, through the benefit of my awakening many years later, that this was probably the first unpleasant event involving "strangers" that I brought into my life. The little girl and the woman involved in the incident were simply "teachers" who mirrored my "feelings" of being alone and innately joyless and reflected them straight back to me. It was, therefore, my first lesson regarding the absence of happiness in my life. Yet not the last. I was to encounter many more interactions with people, big and small, in this regard – but only up until such time as I began to awaken the sleeping joy inside of me by experiencing the "feeling" of connection with my Maker and my inner spirit once more. This in turn has enabled me to slowly recapture the effervescence of life and to once more experience happy encounters with others just as I did as a baby – instead of the sad opposite. Even within large groups.

# Part 2

# Learning About Life

# Chapter 4

# The Messiah of Baby Products

My first awareness that some babies on Planet Earth are considered more perfect than others was revealed to me many years after my birth when working in an advertising agency as a copywriter on a baby products account.

'I've got a "bonus brief" for you girls.' The account director informed me and my art director of this as he bounced into our office holding a larger than normal document. Most briefs, with the exception of new business ones, were single page affairs offering the minimum of information – from which creative teams were expected to produce exceptional ads and campaigns that clients would immediately "love" and identify as being exactly what they wanted. In reality, due to insufficient information contained in these inadequate documents we always ended up creating countless concepts before arriving at one that eventually pleased them. By that stage the approved concept was not, generally speaking, the most creative one we'd come up with and mostly didn't please us, the creative team, anywhere near as much as it pleased the clients.

He continued, his excitement building. 'As I mentioned last week, when they approved your campaign at last, the clients have been researching the distinguishing features of the perfect baby for some time now and have finally come up with a blueprint.' He beamed with enthusiasm. 'This document you see before you lists *all* the characteristics attributable to the perfect baby. Now you can be in no doubt that you've identified the right one when making your choice for the shoot.' My art director and I looked knowingly and less enthusiastically at one another. We realised only too well that this so called "Blue Print", instead of being designed to make our lives easier, was about to place even more pressure on us. Heaven help us if we didn't come up with a "model baby" who matched *all* the recommendations of the clients.

Hordes of mothers beat a path to our casting sessions with an assortment of babies. This one had the right shaped face but the wrong eyes. Another had the perfect smile but was too thin. Then there was the one with the perfect nose but imperfect ears … and so on and so forth. One way or another, and as anticipated, it wasn't proving that easy to find the perfect baby who met all the prescribed criteria. Until, and this wasn't in a casting session, I happened to see him by pure chance late on a Saturday afternoon at my then-husband's tennis club. 'Who is that couple who've just walked past with that beautiful baby?' I declared to the gathering at large. Not waiting for an answer, I got to my feet and swiftly made straight for the couple and their gorgeous child lying gurgling in his pram. As far as I was concerned I'd just discovered the "Messiah of Baby Products". He appeared to be the perfect baby, the one who, as far as I could see, matched all the criteria set out by our clients.

The thing is, though, and with all due respect to the baby products company, I now know that all babies are perfect. I, by way of example, was no exception. Once I'd got over the anxiety of being separated from Shirley so soon after my birth, my early babyhood turned out to be an extremely joyful experience. I was living totally in the 'Now' as all babies do. Life then was as it always should be

– utter bliss in the moment. And regardless of whether I was chubby or not or had dark or fair hair everyone appeared to adore me. The reason? Well, quite simply, I was too young and unspoiled at that time to prevent my "inner spirit beauty" from being seen. Instead I let it shine through my soul the way it was intended to do – just as all babies let their inner spirit shine outwards much to their own delight and that of everyone they encounter. It's just the way babies are created, totally divine.

That is why babies appear so adorable, whether they have the predetermined "perfect baby" features decreed by self-appointed experts or not. Being in touch with their inner spirit beauty not only enables them to be happy and content with themselves but loving of everyone around them, and this of course makes it so easy for them and their admirers to reflect love back and forth. This ideal situation, however, doesn't last, sadly, much beyond babyhood for several reasons, some of which will unfold with this book.

The good news is that our inner spirit beauty can be recaptured and once we start "feeling" it again we are automatically able to reflect it outwards once more to happy recipients who respond in kind. From that moment on the essence of the eternally beautiful life of the eternally beautiful is rekindled for us to experience anew.

# Chapter 5

# Me, My Nana, Shirley and They

'No. No. No. I'm not picking you up for two reasons. Firstly, you're not a little baby anymore and secondly when you do sit on my lap you wriggle so much you always end up creasing my clothes, terribly.' My mother's words came as a bit of a shock to me. I had shown love to everyone I'd come in contact with and had my love returned by all. So it wasn't surprising that I'd anticipated it would be just the same with Shirley. After all, our reunion following her return from the nursing home had gone tolerably well, despite comments on my hair and how much prettier I was without my new born baby fat. Yet that special close relationship I'd hoped for seemed destined not to be.

I did come to realise though, around the time of one of my earliest birthdays, that Shirley preferred interacting with adults than with children and that the way in which she spoke to me was the same manner of communication she displayed to all children.

My birthday party was in full swing. Little kids were running around in all directions screaming, shouting and presumably having a jolly good time. I, by contrast, was in the kitchen engrossed in watching Joseph creatively apply the last drops of icing to my cake which was almost ready to be taken outside for the usual candle blowing ceremony. Joseph had crafted an ordinary round sponge cake into the beautiful face and hair of a doll with his clever application of icing and was happily attending to the finishing touches under the approving gaze of my ever-appreciative grandmother.

Nana, Joseph's number one fan, believed that he had an exceptional and completely natural God-given talent for baking and icing. This of course he did. In a different era I'm sure Joseph would have become a famous pastry chef as there was no end to the gorgeous looking and delectable tasting birthday cakes he created for me over the years. I've also come to realise of course, with the passage of time, that although Joseph performed all his tasks well, he excelled in the area of baking and icing. That's because those were the endeavours he positively "wanted" to do with all his heart.

Shirley by contrast observed proceedings from a distance while paging through a magazine and engaging in her favourite pastime. Smoking. Suddenly the kitchen door burst open and a small girl ran inside crying bitterly. 'For goodness sake, what a noise,' said Shirley, 'what on earth is wrong with *you*?'

The little girl managed to reply between sobs. 'That nasty little boy Brucie … he, he popped my balloon. Now, now I'm the only one who doesn't have a bal…loon.'

'Oh good grief,' replied Shirley, while inhaling deeply from her cigarette and then exhaling long and hard, 'you must never let little boys get the better of you. Why don't you just go straight back out there and … and spit in his eye and choke him.' She burst into laughter, well pleased no doubt with her recommendation.

The little girl stopped crying and abruptly left the kitchen.

'Shirley, you should be ashamed of yourself,' said my very annoyed Nana, 'how many times must I tell you not to talk to children as though they were adults. That may be the punchline to the latest joke doing the rounds in your circle but it is certainly not an appropriate comment to be directed at a child. I hope her mother doesn't get to hear about this.'

Shirley laughed uproariously this time … 'Oh don't be such a wet blanket … now that you remind me, I think it was *her mother* who first told me that joke … have I ever told you the beginning?' But before Nana could reply the door opened in a flurry once more and the same little girl reappeared, crying more loudly than before.

'Oh no, and *now* what's the problem,' asked an exasperated Shirley.

'I … I spat in his eye … but … but he never choked.'

'Oh well, alright then,' said Shirley, choosing not to meet the furious stare of my Nana, 'let's go and get you another balloon shall we? You can even choose your favourite colour.' Shirley now looked at Nana hoping for redemption but it wasn't forthcoming.

The little girl, however, no doubt appeased by the notion of choosing her very own balloon, instantly stopped crying and followed Shirley out of the kitchen in an adoring fashion.

***

Fortunately for me my grandmother totally made up for Shirley's difficulty in developing a close and affectionate relationship with me by constantly showering me with love and attention. I, of course whilst still being at that stage of my life where I could demonstrate my inner spirit beauty with impunity, reflected my great love for her straight back. Or was it the other way round? Either way our relationship was perfect.

'What would you like to do for your birthday darling,' exclaimed my enthusiastic grandmother a few years on from the cradle. 'I'm going to take you out for a treat.' We were seated at her dining room table having just finished lunch. She leaned forward to share two alternatives she had in mind for the occasion. 'I can either take you to the Disney Cartoon Festival or the Pantomime. You can choose.

Tell Nana which one you'd prefer.' She smiled and patted me on my head to encourage a reply. I, seated on cushions so that I could see what I was eating, very carefully returned the glass of water I was holding, in both hands, to the table before looking up at her. I answered with a combination of deep inner thought and outer enthusiasm.

'Mmmm. I, I would like to go to, to the cartoon one, and see *Slee…ping Beauty* and … and the, the dwarfs too, in, in the morning … and then,' my eyes lit up with the potential excitement of it all, 'go to the Pantom … ime in the afternoon.' I finished with an encouraging smile accompanied by the clapping of my hands, in the hope she may consider taking me to both.

My Nana looked somewhat taken aback by my reply. 'Really? Well, you must learn, my dear, that you can't have your cake and eat it. It'll have to be one or the other you know.'

'Why? Why do people give you cake, Nana, if … if they don't want you to eat it?' The thought of a big piece of yummy cake having to be thrown away uneaten wasn't nice at all.

'Oh you beautiful, clever child,' cried my besotted and laughing grandmother as she leaned over and wrapped me in a warm embrace. I reciprocated with equal enthusiasm. 'How can I refuse you? It'll be the cartoon festival in the morning and the pantomime in the afternoon.' She continued to laugh with undisguised pleasure.

'And, and, can we have some popcorn there, too, pleeeese?' I always knew when I was on a winning streak with my grandmother but then again, I seldom wasn't.

Trying to recapture the authority of the adult, she attempted to hide her smile of adoration. 'Well, we'll have to see about that, won't we?' And with that comment I knew the popcorn was practically in the bag.

* * *

Once I was out of nappies things began to rapidly change for me.

By contrast with the self-expression my grandmother encouraged in me, Shirley wasted no time at all in teaching me the opposite. How to behave, how not to behave, how to preserve highly valued material objects at all costs, how to please the world with what I wore and said and did and how to wear my hair in a way the world would love.

I felt overwhelmed by it all and wasn't sure to what extent I had to accept, or was able to object, to what was being demanded of me.

I didn't realise then but have come to learn that we always have freedom of choice. That applies to the standards we choose to set for ourselves as well.

We can choose to grow our vibration and the quality of our life by honouring the commitments we made in the hereafter, prior to our return, by learning the lessons we came to Planet Earth to be taught.

Or, if our resolve doesn't prove strong enough to overcome all the deterrents placed in our way as we grow physically, we can choose not to grow in any other way. And remain at the same vibration with which we entered this life.

The first choice is the ultimately rewarding option whereas the latter unfortunately results in us having to repeat the process and return over and over again. A cosmic kind of "Groundhog Day" if you will.

The key to making the right choices during this lifetime is the unconscious guidance we receive from our inner spirit.

* * *

As you may recall, from Bill's comments on the subject, Shirley had an obsession with hair and spent a great deal of her life combing her own, apart from the time she devoted to mine. It's telling that my parents' bedroom carpet needed to be replaced as many times as it did. My mother continually walked a deep path across it – between her dressing table mirrors and the full-length mirror opposite. The mirrors were specially angled to give her a clear view of herself and her outfit from all sides – and of course, her hair, which she attended to endlessly in an attempt at perfection.

* * *

Most of my early morning pre-school preparation revolved around the grooming of my hair by Shirley. It also included me voicing my blatant dislike of the style in which she chose for me to wear it and the rest of the agony that went with it. 'I … I don't want you to do that … it hurts.'

'And how else do you expect me to get these knots out? I have no option but to brush them out.' Shirley would carry on regardless of my objections until they were all removed.

'But … but why does my hair have to be so long?' I always pulled a very "sorry for myself" expression during the knot removals but to no avail.

'You can't expect to have plaits with short hair, you silly girl. Now sit still or this is going to take all day.'

I always felt that Shirley would have got far angrier at my protestations if she hadn't always become lost in the joyful task of plaiting my hair.

'But … but I don't even like my plaits. I *hate* them. All the other girls at school have ponytails.'

'Don't be ridiculous, your plaits suit you perfectly. You look just like a little Scandinavian girl that Daddy's ancestors would be proud of.'

I could never get my head around how what she said about my paternal ancestors could in any way be of interest or importance to me. 'But, I don't know them … so why do I have to make them happy?'

The morning routine with Shirley wielding brush and comb was a daily occurrence during the week *and* weekend, and although I disliked it with a passion, I was powerless to do anything about it. That, however, was until Bill had to go away somewhere for a while and my grandmother came to stay to keep us company in his absence.

* * *

'*Owwch*, that hurts.' I was complaining as usual while not realising that my closest ally was watching events from the doorway to my bedroom.

'Oh Shirley, for goodness sake dear, why don't you just give the poor child some respite from those plaits. It's the weekend, why not leave her hair loose for a couple of days?' So as not to appear too demanding, my grandmother, a diplomat of note, walked into my room and punctuated her comments by giving Shirley a reassuring pat and a smile.

Shirl, however, shook her head. 'Please don't interfere Mum. If I were to do that the knots would become ten times worse – then you'd really see her perform about me removing them. You have absolutely no idea how fine her hair is.'

'Well then, maybe her hair's too fine to be as long as it is?' Nana proceeded to feel the texture. 'Have you ever thought perhaps the time has come to cut it a bit shorter?'

'Oh yes, please, that would be *so* wonderful, then I could have a ponytail like all the other girls in my class. I've been wanting to have my hair in a ponytail for a such a long time Nana.' I jumped up in my excitement and threw myself on my grandmother's mercy while fiercely hugging her.

'Now stop this performance, specially put on for your grandmother, immediately. How many times must I tell you that your hair is your crowning glory. If I were to cut it you'll just look like any ordinary, plain little girl that nobody is even going to notice. As you've just told us, your classroom is littered with such girls all sporting boring ponytails. Sit down and behave yourself.' Shirley was starting to lose her cool. So I quickly sat down again. But before she could resume her task, I burst into tears.

'Oh dear,' said my grandmother, 'she's terribly upset, let's just leave her for a bit shall we while you and I discuss this matter over a nice cup of tea.'

I don't know exactly what was said but not long after the discussion began it ended abruptly with raised voices ringing through the air. The heated exchange was followed a few seconds later by my usually calm and collected grandmother striding back into my bedroom. She was brandishing the kitchen scissors which, to my delight, she used to cut off at least a third of my hair in one fell swoop.

When Shirley joined us moments later the deed had already been done – so it was no surprise that it was with tears and hysteria that Shirley reviewed the outcome of my grandmother's impulsive action. It took her a good few days in fact to recover. I on the other hand was positively over the moon, as that is how I became the proud owner of my greatest desire at the time. A ponytail. Despite this I did wonder periodically whether the world would now view me as very plain and uninteresting without my plaits.

* * *

The biggest deterrent in maintaining our self-belief in our inner spirit beauty, and thereby our ability to reflect it outwards, is our acceptance of what is said to us about us in our formative years. This ultimately determines whether we go through the rest of our lives "feeling" and therefore "appearing" beautiful or ugly. Or sometimes putting up barriers so we don't feel at all. We become more and more dependent on what others say about us and less reliant on our inner knowledge of what we once instinctively knew to be whom we really are; eternally beautiful beings. Once we devolve into experiencing a feeling of total disconnection from our inner spirit beauty, deep down in our "feeling" selves, it makes it almost impossible for us to be totally happy with ourselves and others anymore.

The result is we often spend our adult lives seeking solutions to what we believe is lacking in us, *as seen by others*, instead of simply going within and experiencing once more the feeling of connection with our Maker – an entity that knows we are perfectly beautiful. Always. For that is the way we are created.

Through recapturing our feeling of "belonging" with our Maker we're once more able to re-establish our connection with our inner spirit beauty. Neither of these has actually gone away. It just seems that way until we reach out to them and embrace them once more. That means the real you, the beautiful you, is also still there albeit in hiding and simply needs to re-emerge like a sleeping prince or princess. So that you can take your rightful place right here on Planet Earth, as well as in the hereafter, as an eternally beautiful being.

* * *

Shirley also taught me from an early age "not to touch" anything and everything in sight as there was a good chance that, if I did, something precious would get broken. 'When Ingrid was a toddler,' she would proudly announce to whoever, 'I never ever destroyed the beauty of my home by putting precious objects on top of cupboards and things. After a few demonstrations of what I expected of her, all I ever had to do was give her one of my ultra-stern looks when she put her hand out to touch anything. She would be so intimidated she'd slap her own hand and declare "mustn't touch".' Relating this story always produced gales of laughter from Shirley, but not always, I noticed, from everyone else.

* * *

One of Shirley's favourite toys, although it really belonged to me, having been given to me by a close friend of my grandmother, was an antique farmyard. This prize possession was kept in my toy cupboard by my mother. All its pieces were individually wrapped in cotton wool and packed in shoe boxes to preserve their beauty. Like all my "good" toys, the farmyard had to be carefully unpacked prior to play and packed away with equal care afterwards. It was so tedious an ordeal that I seldom played with it. I also knew better than to allow other children anywhere near it as I was well aware there'd be hell to pay if there were any breakages. It was my painful duty to "police" all children who came to play by ordering them "not to touch". They seldom wished to return unless forced to do so by their mothers.

* * *

Some years later, when I was in my teens, Shirley instructed me to attend a Sunday morning tea for the youngest daughter of the woman who'd given me the farmyard. 'Andrea is now married with a little boy of her own. I thought it would be a nice gesture if we gave the farmyard back to the family, more specifically to this child of hers.'

'Well, fine, give it to him then,' I said, wondering why I had to be involved.

'Certainly not, you're the one who must present it to him in gratitude for all the many years of pleasure it brought you.' "Pleasure" was definitely *not* the word I would have used to describe the stress and fear involved in owning the "farmyard". Nonetheless, I agreed to be present.

He was a typical Dennis the Menace kind of little chap and I could see from the outset that my mother was extremely nervous about his bouncing around amongst her precious possessions. In an attempt to move the tea along, I was urged by Shirley to present the farmyard as soon as possible.

'Look,' I said with as much enthusiasm as I could muster, 'this is a farmyard with beautiful little animals, birds and things for you to play with.' He immediately dived into the shoebox I was holding with tremendous excitement and pulled out one of the cows. With a look of pure delight, he proceeded to break its head off and positively whooped with pleasure at what he'd done.

'Darling, don't be so destructive,' his mother said. 'Play nicely with the animals.'

"Mustn't touch", I noted, was clearly absent from her vocabulary. I thought my mother might be sick on the spot at the first evidence of what would surely be the complete destruction of her beloved farmyard. I also felt a pang of nausea but for another reason. Although not a fan of wanton destruction, I couldn't help thinking that for so many years I'd been prevented from enjoying the farmyard for fear of harming it yet this free-spirited child had got so much enjoyment and pleasure out of it. In just a few seconds.

* * *

Another area of deep disagreement between me and my mother revolved around clothes. This became particularly evident when I reached my teens and started demonstrating my total unwillingness, in that department, to in any way bend to her wishes.

'Oh,' said Shirley, in a manner that suggested a particularly bad smell had just wafted past her nostrils. 'You don't mean to tell me you're wearing "that" do you?' To avoid a looming confrontation, I turned my attention to the fridge – rummaging through it in search of something to take my mind off the evening ahead. I was, after all, about to go on a date with someone I wasn't even sure I liked. I wondered, not for the first time, how I could possibly get out of it … without resorting to suicide and ruining Shirley's life. Not by my suicide, of course, but by its consequences – the inevitable cancellation of the date.

She drummed her fingers on the countertop. 'I see. I'm going to get the silent treatment am I?'

I shovelled a spoon of fruit salad into my mouth. Considering Shirley and I had opposing views on almost everything, but most of all on hair and clothes, her comment hadn't been totally unexpected. *So why*, I asked myself, *do I always allow what she says to push my buttons?*

'Well,' she added, murdering her cigarette in a perfectly innocent looking ashtray that just happened to be sitting on the kitchen table minding its own business, 'with a bit of luck you'll manage to spill that fruit all over yourself and have to change into something more attractive. Why are you eating anyway? I'm sure this function is a fully catered affair.'

*Uh oh.* I decided the best way to handle a situation that was promising to turn nasty was to take myself and my chosen snack to my room. Shirley, however, wasn't going to be fobbed off that easily. She resolutely followed close behind. All the way into my room in fact, a place that was supposed to be my safe haven.

'Do you know how many girls would give their eye teeth to be invited out by Richard Pringle? The least you could do is take a little more pride in what you're wearing. I can only assume you've chosen to forget who the Pringles are. And why? Why, Ingrid? Just to spite me perhaps?' She suddenly lurched at me, her fingers closing in on my bowl of fruit salad.

'What are you doing?' I screamed with indignation.

'I'm relieving you of this until such time as you become fully engaged in our conversation. And stop lolling all over your bed. Can't you sit on a chair like a normal person?'

First my fruit salad had been confiscated, I couldn't help wondering what would be next. How long before my bed suffered the same fate?

Maintaining her hold on my bowl with one hand, she deftly lit her next cigarette with the last. 'Aren't you worried about creasing that awful dress?' She muttered out of the corner of her mouth without dislodging her cigarette from her lips.

'For goodness sake, I'm wearing the same kind of clothes I was wearing the first time I met him … and I've no reason to believe he didn't approve then.' I made an unsuccessful lunge at retrieving my stolen bowl from her iron grip.

'Oh really? I didn't know you'd met at a funeral?'

'Ha ha … very funny – you know very well it …'

'I don't care where you were, Ingrid, but I do care about where you're going – to a fashionable party at the Country Club with one of the most eligible boys in town. And if you're at all concerned about how you look, you should be interested to know …' Shirley sniffed despite not having a cold '… that they say black is definitely *not* a colour that should be worn by young girls …' *Oh no, not again*, I thought.

'They also say that if it *has* to be worn, that it should be offset with colourful jewellery. So as not to make one look like a grandmother instead of a seventeen-year-old, but more importantly …' Shirley was on a roll '… you might also be interested to know only the brightest colours are being worn this summer. Yellows, pinks and oranges are all "in". Black simply doesn't feature. Why, I keep on asking myself, do you always have to be different? What have I done to deserve a daughter who chooses to make herself look as ghastly as possible?'

I sighed with resignation and closed my eyes, making my head comfortable on my pillows, while bracing myself for yet another lecture on the opinions of the knowledgeable "They". As well as on Shirley's ongoing disappointment in my appearance. 'How many times have I told you, they say you only get one opportunity to make a favourable impression. Heaven knows what Richard and the Pringles are going to make of you dressed like the black widow.'

Eventually and apparently exhausted by her tirade, Shirley finally collapsed into a chair. From the corner of my eye, I detected a slight relaxing of her hold on my fruit salad. This made my second attempt at retrieving it as successful as my response. 'Well I don't care what they say. Okay? I must've already made a favourable impression, otherwise … otherwise he wouldn't have invited me out in the first place. Would he? But sorry to tell you, I'm not that keen on him anyway. He's got creepy eyes.'

With a deeply felt sniff followed by an equally deep sigh and her eyes turned heavenward Shirley departed my bedroom in total exasperation.

* * *

Our differences regarding clothes was to prove to be a serious bone of contention for Shirley throughout her life. Her displeasure was felt particularly acutely when I entered the advertising industry in a creative capacity and where ultra casual and off-beat clothes were not only accepted but expected.

I had arrived to visit her, following yet another bad fall she had just experienced, at the Retirement Village where she was living, and found the newly appointed matron of the village also to be visiting and sitting at her bedside. As I walked through her bedroom doorway, Shirley, covered in bruises and bandages, nevertheless managed to excitedly exclaim, 'Oh matron, here she is, my beautiful, darling daughter, whom you haven't met as yet. She is extremely clever and talented you know. I'm sure you're aware of all these advertisements one sees on television?'

'Oh yes,' replied the polite and slightly confused matron.

'Well Ingrid wrote them you know.' Shirley beamed at the matron who looked as stunned as I felt by this unbelievably incredible revelation. I was in fact an advertising copywriter at the time enjoying moderate success that did not extend to writing every commercial on every TV channel. Shirley, however, who was never completely sure what I did for a living, continued in her quest to impress the matron. 'She's always made us so proud, you know, with what she's achieved in her short life and no doubt she will continue to do so. And matron, she added, you have absolutely no idea how much she earns.' Following on from this embarrassing list of my achievements and attributes to this perfect stranger, she then leaned over very conspiratorially and spoke to the matron just above a whisper. 'But you really must forgive the way she dresses.'

Anyone hearing Shirley's description of me to the matron may be forgiven for thinking that although she disapproved of my style of dress, she surely held me in exceptionally high esteem in every other regard. Wrong. My mother only ever listed what she thought might be considered as admirable about me to others; her friends, our family members and perfect strangers. In other words, those she hoped to impress by reassuring them, in case they thought otherwise, that I was well on my way to becoming one of "They". She never ever told me directly that she thought I was clever and beautiful or that she was thrilled by my achievements. In fact, if truth be known, she really wished that I had embarked on a more "acceptable" career. One that most people would have knowledge of and therefore be "more" impressed with.

In fact Shirley's abiding comments to me and sometimes to Bill, about me, were almost always, by contrast, unfavourable. 'Bill', she would say on occasion when she thought I was out of earshot, 'Did you see what she's wearing? It's hard to believe she wears those kinds of clothes to work and actually gets away with it.'

Other comments directly addressed to me constantly revolved around the fact that if I could be slimmer, but not too thin, better dressed, i.e. in her style of dress (preferably twin set and pearls), and better groomed, I could become reasonably attractive. In fact it was Shirley's abiding belief throughout her life that provided I made a complete appearance change, there was always an outside chance that I could become a leading role player in the hierarchy of "They".

* * *

Our disconnection from our true selves isn't sudden. As we slowly but surely become products of our environment during our developmental years it becomes understandably difficult to maintain our connection with our inner spirit.

Whatever information children are fed by parents and other "teachers", be they family, friends, siblings, schoolteachers, nannies or whatever, is almost certain to be what we grow up to believe.

What other sources of reference do children have? They can't read about "inner spirit beauty" until they've learnt to read and once reading they're still unlikely to search the Internet or attend workshops on the topic. After all it's not exactly a subject that gets much publicity.

It's therefore not surprising that we start feeling and experiencing a whole new set of beliefs about ourselves, courtesy of our "teachers". These beliefs are mostly the unfavourable ones we've been subjected to and as a result the ones that adversely affect us the most.

When we're finally mature enough to start exploring the meaning of life, we're already adults, carrying around all the inadequacies and insecurities bestowed on us by our teachers. I for instance grew up feeling acutely insecure as I became more and more aware of Shirley's unhappiness with me and my appearance. This feeling of inadequacy was further intensified by Shirley constantly looking for guidance on how to change me into how she wanted me to look and behave. From those she revered the most. The ones she considered capable of making or breaking one's success in life – those "gods and goddesses of knowledge" who she always referred to as "They".

This was because she was largely ignorant of the fact, as I was at the time, that she and I had been perfectly created by our Maker with all the benefits that go with it. As a result, she was completely off-track in her belief that the only way to get exactly what she "needed" in life for herself and for me was through the dictates of "They".

The truth of course was that "They", unlike our Maker, who I've only got to know really well in later life, were entirely powerless to achieve her desires. Or mine for that matter. "They", however, were all members, by my mother's decree, of that special elitist club known to her as "the beautiful people". By virtue of that status it was assumed by her that "They" could achieve anything and everything their hearts desired. What's more, provided everyone else blindly followed their dictates, they too could glide effortlessly through life smug in the knowledge that everything would be perfect in every way. Forever and ever, amen.

It was no doubt Shirley's dearest hope and desire that I would become one of "They" as soon as possible, by adhering to their advice on how I should look and live without question.

# Chapter 6

# Abandoned

'Don't leave me. Don't leave me all alone. Don't go away. What did I do? I'll be a good girl. Just come back. Please, please … please come back.' My screams were loud enough to wake the dead but presumably not quite loud enough to wake Shirley. Bill, however, was always a light sleeper.

'Wake up Ingrid, wake up darling. You're just having that same awful nightmare, all over again.'

I, however, was disorientated, caught somewhere between my dream state and the present moment.

'Come on now, sit up and … and have some water.' Bill poured a glass from the jug next to my bed.

I was seven going on eight at the time and I'd been having these nightmares for some years now. It was always the same, and I was always left with a feeling of terror.

'I, I'm scared,' I mumbled to Bill between sobs and gulps of water from the glass he held to my lips.

'No need to be scared. It was a long time ago, you were much younger then. You're a big girl now.'

'But …'

'I've told you before, what happened then is not going to happen again, so no need to worry. Alright? But, you do seem a little chesty?' Bill put his ear to my chest. 'Don't you think you need a puff of your pump?'

'Mmmmm.' I nodded in agreement. The concern Bill always showed about my asthmatic condition was reassuring. Truth be known, I probably didn't really need a puff, but if having one meant he'd linger a little longer and fuss over me, I was happy to oblige.

'Where's your pump? Don't you keep it here on your bedside table? What've you done with it Ingy?'

'It's here, under my pillow. Mummy says it's the best place to keep it in case I need it in the middle of the night when everyone's sleeping.'

'Well come on then, sit up straight and, and I'll hold it while you inhale. There you go, now you can get back to sleep … hmmm?'

'Are you going to go away now and leave me?' I was in fact hoping he wasn't going anywhere.

He patted my head. 'You're going to be just fine, I need to get some sleep too you know. I've got an early start tomorrow.'

'Can't you stay, stay here and sleep, in case I need another puff, later?' Bill smiled but shook his head as he pulled my duvet up around me. 'But, but I don't want to be, all alone.' I sank back against my pillows and instinctively put my thumb in my mouth.

'Now you know you're not supposed to do that, don't you? Only little babies suck their thumbs, not nearly eight-year-olds – right?'

'I, I get scared when I'm on my own.' I'd taken my thumb out of my mouth to reply but had to fight the impulse to put it back.

'Well, you're not on your own. Your mother and I are just down the passage. I'll leave the door open, so you can call if you need us.'

'Can you, can you leave the light on, too?'

'That I can do.' Bill busied himself with switching the main light off and my bedside lamp on. 'Now settle down like a good girl and get back to sleep. It's over now. You'll have forgotten all about it in the morning. Okay then?'

'O … kay,' I replied somewhat hesitantly as I buried my head in the pillows, but as for forgetting about it, I doubted if that would ever be possible.

* * *

As I started to emerge from a deeply troubled and restless sleep, I became aware that I couldn't see any daylight anywhere. Never-ending darkness covered me in a suffocating blanket. I'd never ever felt this alone and afraid. What was even more frightening, however, was the sudden realisation that I wasn't in *my* bed. The mattress I was lying on was much harder. So were the pillows.

I sat bolt upright in terror, wondering just where I was and, at the same time, brushed up against something very hard and cold. That's when I started to scream. I was now shivering from head to toe as I hugged myself to myself to prevent accidently touching "it" again. Suddenly a light cut across the room. It was bright and sharp, and it was held by a woman, dressed all in white, who reflected still more light. It illuminated me and the narrow cot I was occupying as well as the cold metal bars that surrounded it on all sides.

I was immediately wide awake as the memory of being brought to this place the previous afternoon flooded back to me.

* * *

I was about five and a bit years old when I was hospitalised for two weeks for a so-called "Asthma Cure". The fact that I was left in that strange place for that length of time was of course bad enough for a little tot as I was then. Yet to add insult to injury the doctor in charge of the "cure" programme also instructed my family not to visit me during the period. He believed their presence on a regular basis over the two weeks would *upset* me.

Hello? Asthma is supposed to be a stress-induced, fear-based condition that produces a constriction in the sufferer's airways, causing a feeling of not being able to breathe. So being deprived for such a long time of the presence of all those I knew simply increased my fear and associated inability to breathe. The complete opposite of what the so-called "Asthma Cure" was intended to achieve.

But I didn't know any of that then of course. All I felt, for the first time in my life, was that I was *completely* alone in a world that I'd never occupied before. No Shirley, no Bill, no Nana and no Grandfather. This was a different world – one with mean nurses and sobbing children. Children I didn't know and didn't want to know.

It was like living in a very bad nightmare which got worse every time I woke up. When I wasn't asleep, I lived in a constant state of fear wondering if the torture would ever end. *Am I going to be all alone forever? Will anybody ever come and rescue me? When are these strangers going to hurt me again? Or try and make me eat food and take medicine that makes me feel sick? Most importantly, why have I been dumped in this place with these scary people in the first place? What awful thing have I done to deserve it all?*

I constantly peered down the passage, through the bars of my cot, trying to keep my eyes focused on the entrance to my ward – from where I hoped my family would suddenly appear. I watched and I watched, but it never happened. Other people came and went but never *my* people. As much as I thought about it long and hard, I just couldn't for the life of me work out what I'd done wrong. *How could I have been so naughty that I needed to be sent away without a word? Not even one from my beloved Nana who said she loved me more than all the sweets, cakes and chocolates in the whole wide world?*

Whenever the emptiness inside of me became too much to bear I would go over all the reasons why they could possibly have decided they didn't want me anymore – just in case I may have missed the vital reason.

'Don't pretend you don't know I'm here.' The horrible old nurse with the yellow teeth interrupted my thoughts. I felt sick at the sight of her and the mobile tray of frightening needles she wheeled around the ward and that was now parked at my cot. 'It's time for your injection, little miss nasty, and if you try and pull away, as you did yesterday, I promise you it will only hurt that much more.' The sides of her mouth curled into a self-satisfied smirk while the coldness of her eyes revealed the true pleasure she was deriving from the fear her words were inflicting on me.

'You're naughty and I don't like you and your teeth are ugly and yellow.' My responses weren't new to her. I repeated the same or similar whenever she came near me. She never failed to respond in kind.

'I assure you, you little brat, that the feeling's entirely mutual.' Sometimes she even added a few other things she didn't like about me or that she was going to do to me. 'You are without a doubt the naughtiest child in this ward. I don't believe your family have ever attempted to discipline you. But, be sure of this, I'm here to teach you a few lessons you'll never forget.'

That was when the tears came. 'Where are they? When are they coming to take me home?' I always felt the fear and acute aloneness a little more intensely in her presence.

'I have absolutely no idea where they are and who knows if they'll *ever* come back for you? I wouldn't if you were my child.'

She appeared to select my needle from her tray with mounting pleasure. 'Come on then, bend over, I haven't got all day you know. Do you want me to call Nurse Smith?'

After the ordeal of the day before, when she'd got the very large Nurse Smith to hold me down while she injected goodness knows what into me, I decided, just for a change, to give in without a fight.

‘There you are.’ She yanked my nightie back into place. ‘Now you can carry on looking out for your family who, I assure you, won’t be coming for you today. Or probably any other day.’

I bit down on my lip to try and stop the fresh tears I felt forming in my eyes – not so much in response to the sting of the injection on my bottom but because of the pain her words caused me to feel deep down inside. Life with my parents had been strange in many ways but life at this place was like living in a horror movie on a loop. Fortunately I was now starting to feel drowsy from the injection. I decided to give up my vigil behind the bars of my cot, for a little while at least, in favour of escaping into a world of sleep. Who knows, I thought, as I drifted off, if the night nurse finds me sleeping she might not wake me up to eat another horrid meal.

But no such luck.

* * *

‘Come on,’ she said with undisguised irritation. ‘Wake up. It’s time for your supper. And if any of it ends up in your cot, I’ll make sure you sleep in it tonight.’

The night nurses were as lovely as “old yellow teeth” and all the other “child unfriendly” day nurses who proliferated our ward.

None of them cared that most of the resident children couldn’t stomach the hospital food. I could only imagine it was because every meal consisted largely of the same revolting pumpkin mush.

Like me, the other children also vigorously resisted the tasteless fare and cried themselves to sleep after having it force-fed to them, daily.

The only thing the nurses seemed to care about was that more of the mush seemed to end up in the cots, instead of in the occupants, which always made them extremely cross. No doubt because it was something they were responsible for cleaning up.

I personally found the nauseating smell of the stuff the most disturbing. It lingered with me, for many moons to come, making it impossible for me to eat pumpkin again throughout the remainder of my childhood and for many years into my adulthood. It's still not a favourite.

What was even more disturbing, although I seemed to have been at that horrid place for so long, was there was no improvement in my asthma – in fact if anything it seemed worse, not better. I overheard the doctor saying as much to a day nurse.

Yes, I know doctor, but as we've told you she constantly refuses her oral medication.'

'I'm tired of hearing that – have you tried mixing it up, *as I've told you*, in, in some ice-cream or something?'

'Yes, but, well, she's not eating either doctor. All she ever does is spit out almost everything we try and give her to eat.'

'Well set up a drip then. We'll have to start feeding her intravenously … and include her meds in it. I want to be kept informed of her progress on the hour.'

The drip was nice. I no longer had to eat the nasty food. I also felt a bit stronger and it was becoming easier for me to breathe too. Yet, as my strength returned, my spirits weakened. After what seemed like an eternity of fervent hoping for the return of my rescuers, my family, I almost began to believe what "old yellow teeth" had told me. Nobody was ever going to come and take me away from this place. Even worse, I started to wonder if I'd ever really had another home before this one. Perhaps I'd just invented something I wanted to be real.

* * *

I had of course experienced a form of abandonment, otherwise known as separation anxiety very briefly when I was estranged from

Shirley shortly after my birth. But that paled by comparison with the intense abandonment I was enduring at the hospital. Although still very young, I was no longer the happy little baby who was adored and loved by all. And vice versa. I'd already started to become a product of my environment.

Also, as a result, I had moved away from the security of the very positive inner world. A place where my inner spirit beauty and reflected outer beauty had insulated me from the negative influences of the outer world. By contrast with the positive reality of the inner world, the outer world is a place where, feeling disconnected from our Maker, we are constantly exposed to a multitude of false realities represented by negative thoughts, actions and experiences.

* * *

As I lay in my cot attached to my intravenous drip, I began to think that I must have also imagined that once upon a time I'd had a Nana, Grandfather, Mother and Father. Or maybe they had existed but were now dead. I also began to think how it must feel to be a little orphan.

I stopped watching the entrance.

I barely allowed myself to even consider that I may have had a life other than the present one.

And it was then that they appeared.

It was so unexpected I almost didn't believe they were real.

They seemed to be running down the passage towards my cot, some with arms outstretched, my Mother, Father, Grandmother and Grandfather.

'It's me Ingy, it's Daddy darling, look what I've brought you.' He seemed to think his gift was going to make it all better as he held out a giant green sucker, with the face of a clown embedded in it, in red. I'll never forget it.

'Oh my God,' said my grandmother, covering her mouth with her hand, 'she's lost so much weight. How could this happen?'

Shirley was equally concerned. 'And so unkempt. My poor child, it looks as though nobody's bothered to comb her hair or change her nightie since heaven knows when. It seems to be splattered with dried pumpkin.'

She turned up her nose in revulsion.

'I think I'll go and find the Matron,' said my troubled grandfather obviously hoping for answers.

In just a few sentences they were able to confirm for me that they were one hundred per cent real, certainly not figments of my imagination.

Everything they said and did identified them individually and confirmed they were without doubt all members of my family and that they had at last come to rescue me and take me home.

I didn't greet them with cries of joy, though. Disbelief was followed by a non-stop flood of tears of relief and a deep-seated fear that they may go away again sometime soon leaving me once more at the mercy of the terrifying occupants of the hospital.

* * *

What I didn't realise, as our family car left the hospital grounds, was that the damage I'd sustained during my stay there would be going home with me. I had already bought into the false feeling of abandonment big time. It had taken up permanent residence in my psyche and continued to live there, producing ongoing nightmares, for many years to come.

Abandonment, I have subsequently learned, is a condition that produces feelings of extreme fear and anxiety. Someone who fears it will often prefer to sabotage and abandon relationships before the relationships can abandon them. It makes the sufferer feel less vulnerable and more in control. I now realise that this form of the condition certainly applied to my early adult life, and my relationships with men in particular, which will reveal itself in a future chapter.

Alternatively, if in a very repressive relationship, the sufferer may choose to remain in it long past its sell by date, for fear of being alone. That definitely applied to my marriage which will also be visited during the course of this book.

The good news is that abandonment isn't real, even if it feels real at the time. It comes about when we unconsciously lose our connection with our Maker and thereby allow bad feelings to replace good ones. Our Maker is pure love and can only identify with positive thoughts, feelings and experiences, never the negative opposites. When we experience a feeling of separation from the love of our Maker, and as a result the separation of love from ourselves, we naturally feel fear, the opposite of love, very strongly and believe it to be real.

It's only been in recent years following my awakening that I've been able to go back to the hospital, in my mind, and re-live the nightmare. By returning to that ward without fear I've been able to pick up and comfort the deeply distressed little girl, tell her that she was loved then and will always be loved and has never ever really been abandoned. As well as reassure her that now she is fully re-united with the reality of the eternal love of her Maker, there's not the slightest chance of her experiencing unreal feelings of abandonment ever again.

# Chapter 7

# Needing and Wanting

Just like everyone else I had my fair share of needs at different stages and ages while I was growing up. I also had a lot of Shirley's needs and the needs of others foisted upon me too. Needless to say they were all poles apart.

* * *

'You *need* to get up earlier Ingrid. I've never heard of a child who prefers to sleep in late instead of getting up early to make their play days as long as possible.' I suppose Shirley was right. In retrospect I have observed that children in general do seem to like getting up at the crack of dawn to start playing as soon as possible. But not me. I've loved sleeping in for as long as I can remember. Then again I've never liked going to bed early either – even as a little child. 'Ingrid what are you doing in here? How many times must I tell you that you are not allowed to switch the light back on once *I've* switched it off. Now get back into bed and go to sleep – you can't be late for nursery school again tomorrow.' Shirley had no idea that it was my greatest desire at that time to sleep in so late that I could miss nursery school altogether. I was four years old and couldn't imagine a less pleasing place to be at the first light of day.

* * *

I have of course gone through stages in my life when I've tried to develop a personal *need* to get up early to suit societal *requirements* but always ended up feeling exhausted the entire day. Particularly when I didn't get to bed early the night before. I have, therefore, been forced to come to the obvious conclusion, although it's taken me most of my life and the benefit of my awakening to acknowledge, that I do not *need* to get up early because I don't *want* to.

I was obviously obliged to toe the line in this regard as a child, a student and first-time employee. I even felt guilty for arriving late during my early years in advertising, prior to my enlightenment, when I would work late into the night but still be expected to be at work early the following morning. But in recent times I've managed to arrange my life in such a way that I've been able to make provision for sleeping in late. Without the guilt.

For instance I no longer accept or make early morning appointments. Unless it is totally unavoidable. In those rare cases I force myself into bed early the night before with the help of a mild sleeping aid. I also never book flights that leave early in the morning, only day flights from 11am for me. I also work civilised hours and that means never early in the morning but longer hours in the afternoon and sometimes late into the evening or even into the night when necessary. Business breakfasts are out unless there's no alternative. Yet brunches are definitely in. In fact they're my favourite. In essence I have not only given myself permission, but the freedom too, to be me and to do what I *want.*

* * *

'You *need* to take more care of your hair Ingrid. I plait it beautifully every morning but you look as though you've been pulled through a bush backwards by the afternoon.' I was eight years old and Shirley and I had engaged in this conversation many times before so there was nothing new regarding my response.

'What I *need* is to have my hair cut so it doesn't get hooked on things. And so that the other girls at school can't pull on it like they always do. I hate these plaits. Please, please I *need* to have my hair cut more than anything else in the whole world.'

Shirley shook her head. 'And as I've told you repeatedly, I am not cutting it. You *need* to be grateful for your plaits and to look after them. And that's that.'

Fortunately, as revealed to you in a previous chapter, my hair was eventually cut. The underlying reason for this, however, was not solely due to my grandmother taking pity on me. It was because of something I only fully understood following my awakening and which will be revealed in this chapter.

* * *

Miss Jackson, our PhysEd. teacher, addressed me without looking up. 'If, as usual, you're not participating today Ingrid, you *need* to at least make yourself useful. Go outside and make sure the other girls keep on running around the hockey field until such time as I've finished marking these papers.' I replied in the affirmative but in a dejected manner. I knew how popular I was going to be by giving instructions from the sidelines while the others had to keep on running round and round the field in the cold of a winter morning.

'Miss Jackson says you must just keep on going round until she's finished marking some exam papers.'

'Teacher's pet, teacher's pet.' This was their war cry, interspersed by the sticking out of their tongues at me that they all chanted on every lap when they approached the stand on which I was unhappily sitting.

* * *

'I desperately *need* to be able to play sport.' I was sharing my *needs* with Shirley once again. 'Please, please just say I can. I promise I won't get sick. I promise, I promise, I promise. Miss Jackson, our Phys.Ed. teacher, says it'll be good for me.'

Shirley was busy arranging a vase of flowers and didn't welcome the interruption. 'Don't be so ridiculous, how can you possibly promise not to get sick? It's like me promising that the sun won't rise tomorrow morning ... utterly ridiculous …'

'But … you don't understand…' I had tried to interrupt her to explain that not participating in sport was making me, now nine years old, very unpopular with my classmates. But it was going to be a few years longer before this desire of mine would be realised.

'No buts,' said Shirley, 'I've told you dozens of times that Dr Smithers says over exertion will be bad for your chest. If Miss, whatever her name is, keeps bothering you, just refer her to me and I'll remind her of Dr Smithers' letter. It clearly informed the school that you're an asthmatic and as such will not be participating in any sport in the foreseeable future. Now please pass me that small pair of scissors over there on your way out.' With that comment I knew my plea to play sport had fallen on deaf ears. Again.

* * *

'Oh no, you're developing pimples.' Shirley made the discovery and the announcement while peering at my face with a look resembling extreme distaste. 'How revolting the teenage years can be. You poor thing, you *need* pimple cream.' She took her diary out of her bag. 'I'll book an appointment for you to see a beauty therapist during the holidays – she'll sort you out with the appropriate cream that'll heal and disguise those ugly pimples. But you'll *need* to wear it every single day to ensure its going to be effective so that means at school too.'

'No, no, I can't have it ... I don't need it ... I don't want any pimple cream.'

Shirley looked stunned; any physical enhancement was always a win in her book.

'Why ever not?'

I tried to unsuccessfully explain. 'I ... I'll get into trouble – it's not allowed at school.'

'Well, we'll see about that won't we,' declared a defiant Shirley. 'I've never heard of anything so stupid. Aren't you allowed to take headache pills, either, when you've got a headache?'

* * *

'Is that make-up I see on your face Ingrid?' Our head girl pulled me out of line as I exited the first assembly after the holidays.

'No Fiona, its pimple cream.'

'In that case it's a *tinted* pimple cream and I'm confiscating it. If good old-fashioned soap and water is good enough for the other girls, its good enough for your pimples too. Hand it over.' I took the tube out of my pocket and placed it in her outstretched hand.

'Yes Fiona, thank you Fiona.' A simple act of compliance had ended Shirley's *need* for me to apply pimple cream to my face at school.

* * *

'But you promised I could have a new dress for Sally's party. I *need* it desperately.' I reminded Shirley about her offer one morning after breakfast and was deeply distressed by her apparent change of heart.

She was having an after-breakfast cigarette and another cup of tea and responded by shaking her head.

'When I said I'd buy you a new dress I didn't say another black one. What is this obsession with black dresses, black tops, black pants and black jeans. Don't you have any imagination whatsoever when it comes to clothes?'

'Please, please I *need* this new black dress otherwise I won't be able to go to the party.' I was about to exit the dining room when the conversation first started but sat down again, feeling miserable and wondering what I was going to do now that she appeared to be going back on her word. In fact she wasn't being in the least bit helpful. 'You've already got plenty of ugly black dresses, wear one of those.'

'No, you don't understand.' I flapped my hands and arms up and down in desperation. 'It's a special black dress that I *need.* We're all wearing the same style to the party. It's so we can look the same when we sing our song that we've been rehearsing for our all-girl band.'

Shirley, the singer of note, looked horrified. 'But you can't sing in tune to save your life. You know that.'

I closed my eyes so as not to show my exasperation with her. 'Those of us who can't sing well are going to mime.'

Shirley put her head back and roared with laughter. 'Oh my goodness, now I've heard everything. You're all wearing the same style of ugly black dress so that some of you can mime a song in a band you're hoping to launch?' I tried to ignore her laughter. 'Yes,' I steadfastly replied.

'Well I hate to tell you Ingrid but I do believe this "band" of yours has absolutely no chance of succeeding.'

I however was particularly excited about the formation of the band as I had never been asked to be part of a "group anything" before.

I was also beginning to hope that my self-imposed isolation from groups of people was coming to an end. So I really didn't welcome Shirley pouring cold water on the idea of the band.

She half laughed again. 'This is ridiculous and the worst reason I've ever heard for anyone wanting another ghastly black dress. Well I refuse. I'll buy you a dress in any colour as long as it's not black and that's final.'

Don't you understand Ingrid, I want you to look pretty.' She drew long and hard on her cigarette before exhaling for an equally long period while looking wistfully out of the window – presumably imagining a pretty me to herself. I was forced to take that as an indication that her decision was final.

* * *

'Ingrid, come in here immediately and sit down. You and I *need* to talk.' I had tried to tip toe past the lounge without being noticed but no such luck. 'This is your latest school report …' Shirley waved it in the air as I reluctantly sat down. '… and I must tell you before I say anything else, that you *need* to pull up your socks.'

'I'm wearing sandals,' I said, not necessarily trying to be funny but to deflect from the no doubt unwanted content of the school report I'd been fearing the arrival of all week. She either didn't hear me or didn't want to.

'You *need* to apply yourself. It's the never changing feedback from every teacher you have ever had. They all say more or less the same thing.' Shirley then proceeded to read from the latest report. 'Ingrid is capable of achieving much more but she has no desire to work harder – as long as she just scrapes though, she's happy.' She finished reading and gave me one of her stony looks. 'Well I'd just like you to know that your father and I are as unhappy as your teachers are with your cavalier attitude to your school work. You *need* to start paying more attention to your lessons and we *need* to see a change in your attitude to your marks with immediate effect.'

I stood up and then sat down again as I realised she wasn't finished with me. 'If this doesn't happen there will be no further *need* to buy you the latest sandals as there will be no more outings to the beach … or to anywhere else for that matter. You will spend your free time, instead, studying under my supervision. Now go to your room and reflect on what I have just said.' She dismissed me with a nonchalant wave of her hand.

*Ah hah, so*, I thought, as I almost ran to the comfort and security of my safe haven, *she did hear me say I was wearing sandals.*

* * *

Oh dear. The tirade from Shirley relating to my unremarkable school career was not new. It was in fact why I had tried really hard to develop a *need* to improve my scholastic capabilities. But I now decided, at the advanced age of eleven, what I *needed* to find out more than anything else was just how important high marks really were to me. I already knew how important they were to Bill and Shirley. But to me … well I guess the *need* was not that intense.

I confirmed with myself that if it was, my daily mantra of "My school marks are getting better and better" would have paid off by that stage. Instead, as the horrid old Mrs Marnewick, my present teacher and persecutor, had commented in my report, as long as I could scrape through, I was happy. My interest in English, History and Art made this possible although after six months in her class even they were suffering from less than good marks. As for the rest of the subjects … well let's just say they left me stone cold. No wonder my mantra wasn't working.

* * *

'Ingrid, following your poor mid-year results, I had a meeting with your teacher Mrs Marnewick today to discuss your latest report. And she has strongly advised that you *need* to repeat this year.' The three of us, seated at the dining-room table, had just started our evening meal when Shirley dropped her ill-timed bomb.

'Why are we discussing this now Shirley? I thought we'd agreed that it should wait until *after* dinner?' Bill, ever the pragmatist, knew only too well that Shirley's comment surely signified the premature end of a good meal in congenial company.

'What? But we've just got the results of the end of year exams and … and I've already passed this year … so she can't … she can't make me do that.' I was close to tears as I almost screamed my response while at the same time pushing my hardly touched plate of food away from me in further protest.

'There's no need to over react Ingrid. Mrs Marnewick, who's a really charming woman …'

'No she's not, she's an old *bitch*, you just don't know her like I do.'

'Less of that kind of language please …' Bill interjected but Shirley powered on regardless.

'Mrs Marnewick said that you have mostly battled to keep your marks above pass rate this year and that a repeat of the year will be most beneficial to you.'

'She's a horrible old … (I caught myself before using the same word in the nick of time) … and she's been really nasty to me the whole year. You just don't know how nasty because I haven't told you.' It was at about that point that I dissolved into a full-blown outpouring of emotion and cried my eyes out.

'Oh my,' said Bill, 'I had no idea it was going to be this bad. Well congratulations my dear I don't think I can eat anymore either.'

'Oh what nonsense,' said Shirley. 'Ingrid's not a baby anymore, she should be able to discuss matters of importance in a sensible way. And you Bill need to stop trying to protect her at every available opportunity.'

The whole affair was turning into an absolute circus as I continued to declare my position in between loud sobs. 'Please, please don't make me spend another year with that … that awful, nasty person … I beg of you … I'll do anything you want but don't keep me back with her. Please. Please.' I continued to beg for my life while Bill and Shirley looked on in horror. I'd never had a meltdown like that in my entire life up until then and they didn't know quite how to handle it. Fortunately for me my grandmother was brought in the following day to be the final arbitrator in the matter and as a result some sanity prevailed.

* * *

'Why do you say this teacher of yours has been so awful to you? What has she done precisely? And why, darling, haven't you told anyone about it before this?'

Nana and I were sitting on the swing seat in the garden discussing the situation. I bit down on my bottom lip. It was something I always did when I was nervous. 'I … I was scared'.

'Scared? Why?' Nana took my hands in hers.

'I … I thought she'd be even nastier to me if … if I told on her.'

'Well, that sounds terrible … but you still haven't told me what she's actually done to you dear? Tell Nana, you know you can tell me everything without being afraid.'

I nodded. 'I suppose … she just doesn't like me. That's all. I don't know why.' I shrugged my shoulders. 'If I come back from break even five seconds late, she makes me stand outside the classroom for the rest of the lesson.'

'Yes well,' said my Nana knowingly, 'we're all aware that you're not the best of timekeepers, aren't we?' Despite the serious expression on her face, her comment was accompanied by the very faintest of chuckles. 'You and I have had many discussions about it, haven't we?'

'Yes Nana.' I looked down in a guilty sort of way.

'And teachers by nature put a very high value on punctuality. It's really something you're going to have to work on dear.' I nodded and weakly smiled my agreement to what she was saying. 'Now is there anything else I should know?'

I nodded again. 'If I ask her if I can go to the toilet, she tells me to wait until break. If I get a question wrong in a test, she makes fun of me in front of the whole class. And … (it was all starting to pour out of me like an erupting volcano that'd held back for far too long) and the other day, it was very hot and … and one of the girls, Sandy, had an epileptic fit. She's had them before and … and it's very scary because Mrs Marnewick has to push a special rubber between her teeth so that she doesn't bite her tongue. It's horrible … most of the girls crowd around to watch … but I just want to run away and, and always stand back. At the back of the classroom.

'Oh good gracious.' Nana exclaimed her disquiet as she put her hand over her mouth.

'But after it happened last week, Mrs Marnewick was really nasty to me. She said I'd been laughing while Sandy was having the fit and that I should go and stand outside until I learned to be a nicer child. But I didn't laugh Nana … I didn't laugh … why would I do such a thing? I never want to be nasty to Sandy … I feel so sorry for her.'

The last revelation concerning Mrs Marnewick's obvious dislike of me for reasons best known to herself produced another flood of tears that I couldn't control. It was the second bout in as many days. After my startled Nana had comforted me, she returned to the house and the waiting duo of Bill and Shirley to deliver her verdict.

* * *

They were all gathered around the coffee table in the lounge while I was peeping at proceedings from around the slightly open screen door leading onto the veranda – risking being detected but desperate to hear what my fate was destined to be. Shirley was busying herself with cups and saucers and the pouring of tea while Bill characteristically chewed on the inside of his cheek, seemingly undecided about whether to sit down or survey the garden through the window. I wished he'd sit down as that way there was less chance of me being seen.

My Nana of course was holding the floor. 'I know my granddaughter very well,' she informed them. 'When she's in the wrong she always admits it. But in this case the child is definitely *not* lying. Mrs Marnewick would appear to have taken a dislike to Ingrid for whatever reason or reasons and has made her life an utter misery. Presumably she wants to continue doing so by keeping her back for another year.'

Bill turned his full attention on my Nana by asking a pertinent question. 'But why hasn't Ingrid mentioned this … uh … mistreatment by the Marnick woman before this?'

Shirley interjected in an irritated manner. '*Marnewick*, Mrs *Marnewick*, Bill, why can't you ever get anyone's name right?' I hope you can remember it for the next parent's day. Bill just smiled mischievously, happy he'd got the reaction he'd wanted out of Shirley, as my Nana replied to his question. 'She's a child Bill, and as such she feared retribution. The poor dear was in a very difficult position.'

Bill sagely nodded his understanding and finally sat down at the coffee table as Shirley proceeded to hand out cups of tea. 'Cake for anyone?' Bill shook his head. 'Yes please, looks delicious.' Nana was never one to turn down a slice of cake. 'Good grief Maysie, I can't believe you can eat at a time like this,' Bill commented with a grin. 'I most certainly can. After getting to the bottom of why a child is being asked to repeat a year, having passed her end of year exams, albeit not in grand style but not exceptionally badly either under the circumstances, I'm famished.'

Shirley interrupted. 'As I understand it Mrs Marnewick thinks that Ingrid due to her less than stellar performance this year is going to battle to keep up with the rest of the class and may well fail next year.'

'Well then,' said Nana, 'if that happens she can repeat *next year* but at least she won't be held back by a vindictive teacher who doesn't, from what I can understand, have her best interests at heart. You know dear this cake is really delicious, you must give me the recipe.' Nana placed another forkful into her mouth.

'Of course I will … but … well must we assume then, by what you've said, that you're suggesting Ingrid shouldn't repeat the year?' Shirley was starting to gently ring her hands in agitation. 'If that's the case I don't know what I'm going to say to Mrs Marnewick.'

My Nana lent over and affectionately patted Shirley on the knee. 'You are going to say absolutely nothing to her dear. I am going to have the pleasure of meeting with her and advising her of what *we've* decided. And *why* we've decided it.'

Shirley looked perturbed but Bill started to laugh. 'You mean you're going to tell the old bat that because she's been so nasty to our child we won't be accepting her recommendation?'

'Well I'm not going say so in those exact words of course but I'm certainly going to make it clear that we are aware of why Ingrid did so badly this year. You can both rely on me to inform Mrs Marnewick of the status quo in the most diplomatic way. No harm will be done, I assure you, but she might well be prompted to reconsider before making any other pupil's life a misery in future. I feel sure Mrs Marnewick and I are going to understand one another perfectly.' Nana beamed at Bill and Shirley. 'You know I think I might just have another piece of cake.'

* * *

There was much anticipation in the air and a bit of trepidation too as we all filed into the school hall. It was always the case at the first assembly of the year when it was announced who the girls were, in each grade, who had taken the first three places in the previous end of year exams. The wait was interminable as our head mistress started with the first graders and gradually moved her way up the ladder.

The names of the third and second place occupants in my grade rolled off her tongue in a slow and deliberate manner. This allowed for the normal clapping that followed each announcement before she got to first place. I by that stage of events had resigned myself to accepting that I had just scraped through once more when I heard her say my name, followed by … the magical word … "First". It was such a surprise that I almost forgot what I'd practiced doing if I ever got, by some miracle, into second or third spot. That was to look Mrs Marnewick straight in the eye and smile at her.

I quickly sought her out on the podium where she sat with all the other teachers and when my happy gaze met hers she did exactly what I'd always visualised she'd do. She looked away. In so doing she made my day. What I hadn't envisaged was the stunned look on her face.

* * *

'I don't understand it. Why do you always have to be different?' Shirley was having one of her Ingrid-directed rants as she surveyed yet another unsatisfactory, from her point of view, report. 'One shining moment in a dismal school career and then back to normal. Just scraping through again. Why Ingrid? Why do you go out of your way to disappoint me?'

I decided not to distress myself by retaliating. Instead I moved from a sitting position on the couch to a full-length drape all over it in order to take my medicine lying down. But this seemed to infuriate Shirley even more.

'Is it too much to ask that you sit up and explain to me just how you can come top of your class one year, a year when you were not supposed to even go up a grade because of your dismal performance, and then just nose dive back into your disinterested scholastic ways?' Shirley was about to light another cigarette when she realised she was already holding a newly lit one. 'Where have I gone wrong?' she cried out in anguish while popping the unlit one back into her cigarette case. 'What, I keep on asking myself, have I done to deserve a daughter like you?'

I sat up and stretched. 'Look don't take it personally. It really has nothing to do with you. It's all about me. I promise you.' I was now thirteen and involved in many new interests, like boy watching, that required practically *all* my attention and was decidedly more exciting than making sure I continued to come in the top three at school. As long as I passed that was all I really wanted. Well, to be honest, that, and for my friend Elaine's cousin, Mark, to notice me.

Shirley looked a mixture of annoyed and puzzled. So while she was still in a mildly contemplative state I took the opportunity of leaving her to try and work it out, and headed for the kitchen.

* * *

I had of course been over the moon the year before to discover, at the age of twelve, that I had come first for the first time in my life. And as it turned out, the only time. Being able to happily look Mrs Marnewick in the eye and give her the 'see-I-didn't-have-to-repeat-your-class-after-all stare' was however the ultimate reward, particularly when she had looked away. It was at that point in fact that the penny finally dropped. I had come first because I didn't *need* to. Yet I did *want* to with all my heart. Not in order to prove that I was the cleverest girl in the class with the highest marks, but to feel the sheer liberating joy that restoring my faith in myself and my capabilities brought to my life. Also of course, to show Mrs Marnewick just how worthy I was of moving up and out of her clutches.

I didn't know then, of course, anything about the universe rewarding those of us who truly *want* while somehow not quite understanding the pleas of those who *need.* But I could even then, in my unenlightened state, appreciate that I was experiencing so much more positivity in so many areas of my life. Since my awakening, however, I have been able to look back and fully appreciate the real difference between needing and wanting. That one never works while the other always does.

Needing is a negative emotion that comes from a place of lack and works against the natural flow of the universe. Wanting on the other hand is a positive emotion that comes from a place of plenty and works with the natural universal flow to acknowledge that whatever we want is ours.

To start with I spent many unhappy years hating my plaits and informing myself and Shirley that I *needed* to have them cut off for a variety of unfavouable reasons that made them offensive appendages to me. Yet Shirley's desire for their continued presence in my life was greater, and so the more I declared my negative *needs* for their removal the longer they remained.

Only when I came to terms with *wanting* them replaced by a *ponytail*, something I positively *wanted* more than anything else in the world at the time, could I visualise myself, day after day, sporting the desired pony as well as receiving compliments about how well it suited me.

The positive feelings I started to develop around my ponytail soon overtook all the negative feelings I had about my plaits and paved the way for their demise and the birth of my new highly desirable hairstyle.

* * *

As far as participating in sport was concerned, well I didn't really *have* to play sport at all. Regardless of being labelled as an asthmatic or not I was *never* cut out to be much good at *any* sport. But only when I stopped whining in a negative way about my *need* to participate and concentrated more on *wanting* all the positive aspects of being part of the gang, represented by my sports playing classmates, was I eventually allowed to play. Albeit not very well.

* * *

Ah yes, and then there was the pimple cream. This is a strange one. Obviously like all girls who begin to suffer from hormonal change as they reach puberty, I *needed* pimples splattered all over my face like a hole in the head. But Shirley's insistence that I apply pimple cream to get rid of them came at the very same time the ban on me playing sport had just been lifted. This was following an intervention by Bill who, a sportsman himself, suggested at long last that I be allowed to participate to see, once and for all, if sport would *improve* or *worsen* my asthmatic condition.

Needless to say my lungs were already experiencing the benefits of opening up to fresh air and exercise while my acceptance by my peers was also, as a result of participating in sport, just kicking in at the same time. So why on earth would I *want* to spoil the status quo by being the only girl in the school sporting a pinkish-coloured pimple cream that wasn't particularly attractive or even allowed.

Shirley's desires, however, as you'll recall, proved once more to be greater than mine in this department too. Fortunately, and thanks to the positive feelings I was beginning to experience around *wanting* to fit in with my peers, the intervention by our head girl proved very welcome. It ensured I wore the pimple cream for such a short time that nobody really noticed and my newfound standing with my classmates, that I *wanted* so much, was not adversely affected.

* * *

My request to Shirley for a "special" black dress was also of course something linked to me *wanting* to fit in with my peers. When I was invited to obtain this dress in order to be one of the "back-up mime artists", in what was to become an all-girl band formed by my classmates, I felt an overpowering *need* to acquire it. Due to Shirley's refusal to buy it for me, however, I started *wanting* to be part of the band more than *needing* the dress.

I *unconsciously* started employing the same tactics that had assured me of victory over my plaits, the pimple cream and my initial inability to persuade Shirley to allow me to play sport. So deep was my positive desire in fact that I kept on, day after day, seeing and feeling myself on stage with the rest of the band. And hey presto, guess what happened next? It was brought to the attention of the mother of our band leader, Sally, that I would not be participating due to not having the right dress for the occasion. This in turn resulted in Sally's mother phoning Shirley regarding the matter and all *hell* breaking loose.

* * *

I wondered at first if Shirley had decided to smoke twice as many cigarettes as normal. Smoke seemed to be pouring out of her ears as well as her nostrils. 'How dare you,' she fumed. She was sitting on *my* chair in *my* bedroom. "How dare *you*," was almost my knee jerk response before I thought better of it. After all, her invasions of my private sanctuary, my bedroom, were becoming too frequent by far.

'How dare I what?' That is what I ended up replying as I reluctantly sat down on the chair opposite her.

'You have your faults Ingrid but I never thought I'd given birth to a little sneak. Is there nothing you would not stoop to in order to get this ghastly black dress you are after?'

I was seriously puzzled. 'I … I don't know what you're talking about?'

'Oh yes you do and if you think you're going to get off lightly by saying that you don't, you're sorely mistaken.'

I gave an exasperated sigh. 'Look, I tell you what, I'll say whatever you want me to say provided you tell me what I'm supposed to have done wrong. Okay?'

Shirley sat back and pursed her lips. 'You may be interested to know that Sally Waters' mother called me today.'

'Oh really,' I was surprised. 'I didn't know you even knew her.'

'I *do not* know her Ingrid which makes this whole affair doubly embarrassing. Presumably you complained to her that I wouldn't buy you that dress for this band you, her daughter and whoever are busy forming – which has led her to believe I can't afford it. So she had the cheek to call me to offer to buy it for you provided I'm agreeable.' She lit up again after sharing a huge sniff with me.

'But I've never even met Sally's mother. Maybe Sally told her you couldn't afford the dress. I just told Sally you'd refused to buy it for me so chances of me being in the band weren't great. That's all.

'Hmmm,' said Shirley in a non-accepting manner. 'I'm not sure I entirely believe you but if what you say is even vaguely true you need to word things more clearly in future. So that there is absolutely no chance of misinterpretation. Under the circumstances I've had no option but to inform Mrs Waters that there has been some misunderstanding and as such there's no need for *her* to buy the dress as *I* will be doing so.'

I could just feel the extent of the smile spreading across my face. 'Gee, thanks Mum.'

Shirley closed her eyes in irritation. 'What else could I do? I cannot have untruthful rumours being circulated that I cannot afford to buy my daughter clothes, can I? However, whether you were involved in this stunt or not, I have just one message for you. If even a whiff of an untruth relating to me comes to my attention again there will be serious repercussions.' With that definitive statement Shirley removed herself from my room.

I felt yet another smile spreading across my face as I reclaimed my chair. I wasn't of course guilty of performing any stunt but at the mature age of fifteen I was guilty of feeling pretty happy with the outcome. In fact I felt a whole new world opening up.

I not only became the proud owner of a new black dress but more importantly I also got the peer acceptance I so wanted. By becoming a bone fide member of the shortest lived, all-girl band in history. Just one performance was all it took to launch us and disband us. By popular demand.

* * *

What I learned from all these events in my life, but only fully understood following my awakening was of course invaluable.

The magnificent Universe, also known as God, our Maker, our Creator, our Source and more, and of which we are all part, provides every one of us with a plentiful supply of what we want. So there's absolutely no need to need anything. All we have to do, to ensure we always have everything, is nothing. As long as we're matching the natural flow of the Universe with positive thoughts and actions we'll instinctively know that whatever we want is ours. And, as a result, we'll feel the benefits of having it even before it materialises.

Alternatively, we can decide to operate alone, not as part of the positive universal whole, and in so doing go against the flow. This also means, in effect, going against ourselves by refusing to believe we are all created to have everything we want – and choosing instead to negatively demand our individual needs for things we are actually pushing away by these actions.

# Part 3

# Everlasting Life

# Chapter 8

# Losing the Best Part of Myself

It had to happen at some stage of course but I never even entertained the thought that it would. In fact it was not something that even entered my head until it happened.

When I lost my grandmother it felt as though I'd lost the best part of myself. How, I thought at the time, was I supposed to go on living when only a very miniscule piece of me was still alive? With hindsight I did however have something to be very grateful for during those dark days, following my loss, and that was the fact that I was still a child.

Children adapt so much better to their changing circumstances for a couple of reasons. They aren't carrying as much "life weighing down" baggage as adults and it hasn't been that long since they were babies and fully in touch with their protective inner spirit – so the connection, no matter how weakened, is still stronger than in adults. Both these factors enable children to not only cope better with losses but also to heal that much faster no matter how devastating the circumstance of the loss.

Adults on the other hand, generally steeped in great multitudes of baggage and mostly having forgotten that they possessed a protective inner spirit in the first place, find it incredibly difficult to move on from losses. The loss of precious loved ones in particular.

Children, unless encouraged to keep on mourning, acknowledge their loss and allow themselves to feel it deeply before letting it go. This doesn't mean they never give it a second thought. On the contrary, they're unlikely to ever forget the love of the one they have lost and will periodically express their remembrance with sadness. By the same token they generally don't allow the memory to dominate their lives to the exclusion of everything else that makes life so wonderful and worth living. It has been observed that in the early stages of a loss of a loved one, children can quickly alternate between sadness and happiness with the greatest of ease – not allowing either emotion to dominate.

Adults can therefore learn a lot from children in this regard. Or not. If we decide to learn from them the first thing to do is to consciously choose to reawaken the feeling of love we have for our Maker and as a result for ourselves. Once achieved we automatically open ourselves up to feeling the beauty of our inner spirit once more. This in turn enables us to move on from the loss of a precious loved one that much faster – by feeling a desire to let go of unwanted baggage as we rediscover the healing benefits of relinquishing negatives in favour of positives again. That of course offers us the opportunity to continue to enjoy our life, and all the happiness it offers us, unclouded by just one unhappy event.

# Chapter 9

# Dying to Live Forever

I was crying uncontrollably while sitting on something uncomfortably cold, hard and unwelcoming.

Only when I climbed down from it and read the inscription on it did I understand that I had been sitting on my beloved grandmother's tombstone at her grave site. A place where a great multitude of wreaths and bouquets lay scattered – tokens of appreciation for her life on Planet Earth from all the people who loved her almost as much as I did.

This further confirmation of her physical departure from my world served only to deepen my stress as yet another flood of pain-induced tears fell from my eyes.

Suddenly, however, and as if from nowhere, she miraculously appeared. She seemed to be dressed in a white flowing robe and she looked quite beautiful, totally unlike the emaciated corpse I'd seen lying in her coffin at her funeral. That disturbing vision of her had been the last glimpse I'd had before being gently but firmly ushered away by Bill and Shirley.

Now my beautiful Nana stood before me once more and opened her arms to me, as she had always done and I ran straight into them, this time sobbing more from unbridled joy and relief than sadness, as I wrapped myself around her. I never wanted to let her go, ever again.

She held me and rocked me in a familiar and soothing manner. 'Don't be sad my dearest darling, be happy for me,' she murmured. 'Nana is now living somewhere very special. All the nasty pain has gone away and I am happy again.'

'But I … I don't want you to be dead … or happy without me. And I don't want you to live somewhere else … I want you to stay with me always.' I buried my head in the comfort of her breasts as I had done countless times before.

'I am not dead little Ingy. I, like you, and every one of God's eternal spirits, will live forever. And I will be close to you, at your side, always.'

I wasn't convinced. 'But … but if you are living somewhere else … will I, will I be able to *see* you again … like now?'

She gently stroked my head. 'No my darling but I promise you that you'll be able to *feel* my presence and know that I love you, eternally.' Then, just as suddenly as she'd appeared, she was gone and I, missing the comfort of her touch and visual presence was left bereft again, sobbing loudly once more.

When I woke up my pillow was still wet. But somehow, although I was just twelve years old and I'd only seen her again in a dream state, her words have stayed with me always. With the benefit of time, especially the time following my spiritual awakening I have come to understand and appreciate the positive meaning of everything the dream revealed to me.

# Chapter 10

# Living in the State of Good Health

'Well, am I going to live or is this persistent little cough I've developed going to be the death of me?' Nana had laughed in her normal positive, fun-filled way when her GP had phoned her and asked her to visit him at his rooms to discuss the x-rays she'd had taken at his insistence a few days before. She had also made light of the entire situation when she'd described to us, in detail, what had transpired at the follow-up appointment. My Nana was of the opinion that her GP was totally over-reacting by suggesting a mild, yet irritating little cough was worthy of an exploratory procedure, no matter how minor.

* * *

'I don't want Nana to stay there. I don't like the way it, it smells of … medicine and, and sick people. And … and *she* doesn't like it there either. She told me she wants to leave just as soon as possible.' I was totally miserable as we drove home following my first visit to the hospital to see my grandmother. It reminded me of the awful place at which I had spent some utterly dreadful weeks during my so called "Asthma Cure". But not only that I also knew instinctively that it wasn't the kind of place I'd want my worst enemy to be admitted to, let alone my beloved Nana.

'Of course Nana doesn't want to be there any longer than she has to, and that's why just as soon as she's recovered from her little procedure we'll be taking her home. We'll have a wonderful surprise home-coming party for her shall we? All her favourite people will be invited and all her favourite cakes baked for the occasion. In the meanwhile it'll be something to look forward to.' Shirley was trying to sound as cheerful as possible. Somehow though I could hear, underneath it all, that she was as concerned as I was about the hastily arranged procedure that was due to take place the following day.

Shirley continued to try and reassure me as well as herself. 'I'm convinced there's no need to worry, after all surely her doctor should know what's best for her, shouldn't he?' She asked the question as much of herself as of anyone else but it was Bill who answered.

'No doubt about that darling, besides, it's always better to be safe than sorry – what's more the surgeon who is going to perform the procedure has an excellent reputation so she'll be in the best of hands and back home before we know it.' Shirley had smiled weakly and nodded her agreement while I felt less positive about what was being said with every word uttered.

* * *

The positive expectations, sadly, voiced by the pair of them regarding the outcome were far from what actually transpired. The so-called "wonderful surgeon with the excellent reputation" apparently discovered the beginning of the big "C" on one of the lobes of one of Nana's lungs during the "little exploratory procedure". Instead of sewing her up again and discussing with her whether she wanted it removed or not, he simply took it upon himself to cut out her *whole lung* there and then.

My previously healthy grandmother, who always displayed such a zest for life, became very ill overnight, never recovered from the ordeal of the traumatic surgery and passed away within months of it.

In those days, of course, that sort of thing wasn't questioned that much. It was simply accepted as the norm. Comments like these abounded: "Just as well he removed it before she suffered even more." "She had a good life and sometimes for people as beautiful as May it's a blessing to die young." What nonsense. She no doubt brought the events that led to her demise into her reality for whatever reason best known to herself. But she wasn't really sick when she went for her annual check-up and mentioned a persistent little cough to her GP.

How do I know this? Well, once again, following my awakening I have learned that the body doesn't think for itself. It can't. Only the mind can think. So the only time a body can become terminally ill is when the mind encourages it to believe it's on its way out. Once the body buys into the instruction from the mind, the condition, whatever it may be, is confirmed and the body starts to deteriorate at a rate also set for it by the mind.

Alternatively if the mind chooses to believe that the body will always be in a good working condition, it will.

'Ah but that's not possible,' say the critics. 'We all have to die of something, sometime.' Well, I believe, that's not exactly true either. First of all we never die. We simply give up our bodies at some stage and revert to living as eternal spirit beings, otherwise known as "Light Bodies", which don't have a form but live forever. They are the same eternal spirits that live within our human forms during our lifetimes on Planet Earth.

I also believe that when it is time to return to the hereafter, the place from where we originally come, there's no need to surrender our physical bodies to some dreaded disease, fabricated for us and introduced into our minds either by ourselves or someone else. We can just as easily depart this world peacefully, in our sleep, as so many evolved souls choose to do.

The same would apply to a person's so called "need" for "good health". It is no good whatsoever blaming the Universe for so called "bad health" and demanding our *need* for a reversal of the condition when "bad health" simply doesn't exist. I have already mentioned that your Maker only wants all things "good" for you and therefore only understands "positive" language as opposed to the "negative alternative". Therefore "bad" is not a word in the vocabulary of your Maker. What's more, have you ever wondered how health can be bad? It's a bit like saying someone is ugly beautiful. Health means health. The word speaks for itself.

Also, as we are created perfect, in the image our maker intended, it stands to reason that this perfection would not only include our perfectly designed bodies, features and faculties but the perfect state of our health too. We can of course "experience" the unreality termed by some as "bad health", if we wish, but know that it is not a "real" condition unless we choose to make it real.

Although based on much of what I have learned here and there from other sources, these are my beliefs entirely and if I have offended you by sharing them with you, I'd like you to know it was not my intention and I apologise.

I for instance chose to experience the unreality of a condition known as asthma shortly after my birth. This was no doubt a response to my stressful birth and the equally harrowing experience of it that my mother endured and conveyed to me.

The medical team witnessing my arrival at first believed I was a "Blue Baby". This was until such time as they, in their wisdom, determined that I was, instead, an "asthmatic" who was experiencing my first attack. So I was labelled an asthmatic by them and eventually by everyone else in my world. Going along with their beliefs I too bought into the unreality of this condition for most of life. Was my asthma ever real, though? I don't believe so. I was just experiencing the "unreality" that everyone told me existed within me. A belief so deeply entrenched and fostered in my mind by all and sundry from such a young age and over such a long period of time it has been hard to shake.

Having gained more knowledge on the subject, however, I now realise that although I chose my mother to give birth to me, I obviously wasn't prepared to handle her extreme anguish during the event. Or her feelings of resentment towards me for the pain she was experiencing and which she later came to verbalise as being "torn to shreds". This resulted in me not wanting to take my first breath. Or any subsequent breaths, to escape from being born altogether.

It's ironic for me that the famous spiritual leader and author, Louise Hay, in her highly acclaimed book entitled '*You Can Heal Your Life*' refers to what she terms "Baby Asthma" as "Fear of life. Not wanting to be here".

# Part 4

# Living and Learning More

# Chapter 11

# Lessons in Love

'What? What do you mean you're calling off the wedding? Have you gone completely mad?' The sound of Shirley's anguish and displeasure rang so loudly down the phone that I imagined my eardrums were in jeopardy of bursting.

'You can't possibly – everything's been arranged. How dare you? Poor Gertrude, she must be beside herself with, with worry and … and stress … and ….'

I was holding the phone away from my ear at this point, twirling the line in my fingers and contemplating hanging myself from it … but decided instead to try once more to make a breakthrough.

'Please, can I, can I, at least say something …?'

'Not to mention how Grant and Hugh must be taking it. How can you do this to Grant? What, I keep asking myself, have I done to deserve a daughter like you?' There was no stopping her though. It therefore occurred to me at that point that the phone line might perhaps be better suited to her neck than mine.

'Gertrude and Hugh have gone out of their way to welcome you as part of the family. And poor Grant adores you.'

I could hear her pause to light another cigarette, and leapt in.

'Do you mind just letting me …'

'Bill … Bill,' she shrilled, 'come here and listen to what your darling daughter is up to now … don't just walk away … *urgh*,' she muttered, 'both of you are totally impossible.' Bill was used to being summoned by Shirley to sort out all manner of problems but didn't always engage. He particularly tried to avoid disputes between her and me.

Shirley drew deeply on her cigarette as I quickly ventured a comment. 'Maybe he'll speak to me?'

I had now adopted a yoga type position, lying with my back on the floor and my legs against the wall to help ease the stress of it all.

'Bill,' she cried out once more, 'do you want to hear this or not?' She paused, then sniffed, no doubt to indicate that Bill, very wisely, would not be participating in the call.

'Typical of you, of course, to only be calling me now. Why didn't you phone immediately you started having this ridiculous idea? Instead … instead of leaving it to the last minute?'

'Because, because I knew I'd get the response I'm getting now.'

I was undoubtedly having the worst conversation I'd ever had with Shirley. Thank goodness she was in South Africa and I was in the UK. I was simply hoping, or rather, desperately trying, every time I managed to get a word in edgeways, to somehow justify my actions. The more I tried however, the more it sounded as though I was wilfully destroying everyone else's life in selfish pursuit of my own happiness.

*How,* I wondered, *have I got myself into this mess?* I had done absolutely nothing to deserve it, of that I was convinced, at the time … and yet everything was falling apart.

* * *

The first time I saw Grant was one night at a party. The second time was the following day. 'Ah, found you,' he said. He was sweating profusely under the boiling hot southern sun and a heavy northern hemisphere suit.

I sat upright on my towel, trying to control my laughter. 'You do know this is a beach and not the North Pole?'

'When a man's on a mission to re-unite with the girl of his dreams, there's simply no time to change into a dashing pair of baggies.' He grinned as he sat down, removing his jacket and tie.

'So how did you know I'd be here, anyway?'

'James, the chap whose party I met you at last night? He was the informant. Hope you're not going to hold it against him?'

* * *

Hmmm James, I reminisced, as I watched the English countryside fly past the window of my London-bound train. He was the one who was really to blame for the fact that I was forced to cancel the wedding, ruin people's lives and leave Grant's family home in such a hurry. If he hadn't had that bloody party, I'd never have met Grant in the first place. I thought of phoning Shirley to tell her who the true culprit was, but sensibly decided against it.

* * *

Grant was a British journalist with Reuters – some years older yet madly attractive to me at the time. He had a brief assignment in South Africa, before going on to another longer stint in the East, and we "fell madly in love" as the saying goes.

I was still a student but when he phoned from Singapore to deliver his marriage proposal, I thought nothing of accepting it. 'I feel I can't live another day without you,' he said. 'I'll be back in the

UK for Christmas, what do you say to joining me there for a January wedding?'

'Oh my precious darling,' I exclaimed, a touch theatrically, 'I can't bear being without you either.' In retrospect I believe I was reciting a line from a movie, or was it a play … or perhaps even a romantic novel I'd read. It doesn't matter. What hindsight has cleared up for me is that I was definitely more in love with love than I was with Grant – as well as the idea of travelling overseas and starting a new life in a new country. I'd miss Bill of course but … well Shirley would be happy in the knowledge that I would be living a life that "They" could surely have scripted for me.

* * *

I was right. She was ecstatic. Grant was practically everything she'd ever dreamed of. 'Apart from his having a wonderful career ahead of him, I just love his sense of humour and he's verrrry attractive,' she gushed to a group of her closest tea-sipping friends. 'He's also public school educated, you know, and his family are positively perfect. Gertrude, his mother, is an absolute darling and Hugh is an Air Vice Marshall in the RAF. They've travelled practically everywhere. I couldn't be happier for Ingrid.'

I wondered if Shirley wasn't having an identity crisis. Was she perhaps confusing my happiness with hers?

* * *

I'd always wanted to do a solo sea cruise and thought, in my naivety, that I should take the opportunity en route to the UK – rationalising to myself that it would not be something I could do once I was married. Shirley and Bill thought the idea was decidedly odd and that I should fly, but I discussed it with Grant and it was settled. 'Of course, if that's something you really want to do darling … then do it,' he said generously. 'I don't want you to regret anything. I, I just want you to be happy.'

* * *

It seemed as though every Hollywood movie I'd ever seen about cruises had suddenly come to life. Clear, sunny skies above and endless blue sea surrounded decks festooned with pools, pool loungers and beautiful people. When the sun was replaced by the moon, the stars seemed more breath-taking than I could ever recall – reflecting their magical light off the never-ending ocean. Oh yes, the trip started out as everything I thought it would be … utterly wonderful. But, unfortunately, it became a whole lot more.

I fell in love with 2$^{nd}$ Engineer Harry Collins the moment I saw him standing to the side of the dance floor in his uniform.

'And what's a beautiful young lovely like yourself doing alone on this ship,' he said in his divine Irish brogue.

'Waiting for you to ask me to dance,' I blurted out a little breathlessly. And that was that.

Apart from when he was on duty, we were inseparable. The only problem was that I hadn't mustered up the courage to tell him about Grant. It was eating me up inside. I didn't even know where or how to begin.

* * *

'I've decided,' said Harry, gently stroking my back, 'I'm going to be taking shore leave just as soon as we get to Southampton so we can travel straight on to Dublin and then to Donegal to have Christmas with the family and to pick up my car. Then I'm taking you on a road trip through Ireland you'll never forget. You're going to love

Ireland almost as much as I love you.' He kissed me on the tip of my nose.

'Sounds wonderful, but … but what about my, my other plans … I …' I fidgeted nervously with the sheet.

'I *am* your future plan darlin, and … you're mine … I don't want to even hear about anything you may have planned before we met. Okay?' Harry applied his stern look that made him appear even more attractive.

Shirley would have applauded my rapid weight loss. I could hardly eat a thing as I wrestled day and night with how I was going to resolve the situation.

One thing was for sure, marrying Grant knowing I could have such strong feelings for someone else seemed impossible. Harry was the one, the real McCoy – it was just a coincidence he was Irish.

* * *

I stupidly left it to the very last moment of course.

'Harry,' I said, as we lay wrapped around one another, the night before the ship was due to dock in Southampton. 'Can I tell you anything … and everything … without you ever getting cross with me?'

Harry looked deep and lovingly into my eyes. 'Of course you can my love.'

'Well …' I sat up, took a deep breath and looked agitatedly through the porthole. 'What would you say if I … if I told you I'm … even though I don't want to be … engaged to be married … and my fiancé's meeting the boat?'

I turned to see how he'd taken the first bit, before telling him how much I loved him and how I really wanted to be with him and only him but realised too late that I'd worded everything the wrong way round.

Harry looked as though I'd just shot him with a 12-bore shotgun. He did, however, manage to get up.

'I'm going on duty now … and when I get back I don't want to find you here … do you understand?' He was close to tears.

'No, no … you're the one who doesn't understand … let me finish … I love you. I love you more than anything.' I jumped to my feet and tried to throw my arms around him. I'm going to break it off with him … just as soon as … as I see him.'

'No,' he said pushing me away, 'you've already done enough damage. Go, go … and get ready for the poor bastard. But don't think for one moment I'll be taking his place.'

With that he walked out of his cabin, in a state of half undress, never to be seen again.

* * *

As it turned out, Hugh was the darling but Gertrude … well, she could've been Shirley's twin. No wonder they bonded before even meeting one another.

Yet as far as *my* relationship with Gertrude was concerned … well let's just say fate had kindly stepped in during the cruise to ensure we wouldn't be having one.

* * *

'I hope you'll soon be over your jet lag or sea lag or whatever it's called, Ingrid,' said Gertrude, pouring herself yet another cup of tea. 'We have much to do. Due to the wedding being just around the corner I had no option but to choose your wedding gifts. They've been on display at Harrods since the end of November when Grant first informed me about this wedding. And most have already arrived – so we'll have to go through them ASAP and see if there are any duplicates or … or any you positively hate – which will have to be returned and exchanged.'

She proceeded to set out all my imminent duties at breakfast the day after I arrived but I didn't have an appetite for either.

'Talking of Harrods, I've also selected a few dresses for your nuptials. Christmas is now upon us and the wedding will soon be too. So absolutely no time to have a dress made. We'll go up to London this week for you to take a look see and … and choose.'

'Yes, but … but …' I was trying desperately to swallow a piece of stuck toast that was inhibiting my ability to talk.

'But what dear?'

'I, I actually brought a dress with me,' I managed to defiantly squeak. Although it was hardly worth mentioning as I wasn't planning on wearing it of course.

'Have you? Well, we'll see.' Gertrude took another sip of tea. 'Shirley tells me you have a penchant for the unconventional, so let's just make sure we choose an appropriate dress for the occasion – shall we?'

'Uh, well, I … I.' I bit off another piece of toast in the hope that it too would get stuck. I needed all the help I could get to avoid being rude to Gertrude.

'Today, however Ingrid, we're driving through to Salisbury to change your bank account. We bank with Lloyds so it won't do for you and Grant to bank at different institutions.' With that comment Gertrude stood up indicating we were leaving for Salisbury, this despite the cup of tea in my hand that was on its way to my mouth.

* * *

Grant had left early for a meeting in London so I hadn't yet managed to confront him with the news I was dreading to impart – that I wouldn't be marrying him after all and something which of course made all Gertrude's demands on me purely academic.

The eventual discussion with Grant proved to be so heart-wrenching that I have chosen not to include it in this book. To say he took the news badly would be an under-statement. As a result it turned out to be one of the worst ordeals of my life. But to repeat every word we uttered to one another would serve no purpose other than to reignite the guilt I tried to distance myself from for so many years after the unhappy event occurred.

* * *

As a matter of interest, I did try and contact Harry again – the 'one' I thought was the love of my life at the time. I left a note for him with the ship's purser before I disembarked, recklessly providing Hugh and Gertrude's address. Sadly it produced not the slightest response. Or not as far as I know. As you're aware I wasn't there for long so whether he decided to look me up is not known. Yet safe to say its doubtful Gertrude would've happily provided him with my London address if he'd suddenly pitched up on her doorstep after my departure.

* * *

I now realise, of course, only too well, what chaos I was instrumental in bringing to all the lives I touched at that stage, not least of all to my own. But then, well then, I didn't have a clue about anything much. I was firmly on a path of self-destruction. If I'd known at that point what I know now I could've avoided all the heartache. Then again if I had avoided it, I wouldn't have learned one of the most valuable lessons I'd come to Planet Earth to be taught.

* * *

With hindsight I have come to acknowledge that my relationships with Grant and Harry were simply a prelude to many more unions with a series of Mr Wrongs who I constantly encountered in my misguided search for love and fulfilment.

Initially we believe the very special love that we crave is "out there" somewhere. That is why we seek it desperately in all the wrong places, believing it can only be found in relationships with other people, particularly in sexual relationships with the elusive Mr or Ms Right.

Over and over again we tend to confuse the initial excitement of a new relationship with having found the true love of our dreams. Sadly, however, the initial feeling of euphoria inevitably doesn't last. As each relationship fails we pick ourselves up, dust ourselves off, and begin our search all over again. This we do in the blind faith that our next relationship will be with that special other, and that, once found, it will provide the eternal love and happiness we long for.

We mistakenly believe that then and only then will we feel whole. But the reality is it doesn't take another person to complete us. All it takes is the realisation that we are already whole. Our Maker *is* love and as we are one with our Maker we carry that love within us. Always. It's the love we are born with as demonstrated by our inner spirit beauty that shines so brightly it can't help but radiate outwards when we are babies and in so doing attract the reciprocal love of others.

The good news is that once we've re-united with our inner spirit beauty, through recapturing the feeling of love for our Maker, and thereby the love of ourselves, we can radiate it outwards once more. It is only then that we will be sufficiently secure, open and receptive to experiencing loving and long-lasting relationships with others too.

# Chapter 12

# Judgment Days

I always knew, without a shadow of a doubt, that Shirley was super judgmental. I had after all the unequivocal evidence of this going back as far as I could remember. It was her most difficult personality trait but one that I'd come to reluctantly accept during my younger years. It was also the one that was most evident in her day to day life so it was impossible not to live with it.

It only began to worry me unduly in later life, as I witnessed her group of friends dwindling.

I remember discussing my concerns with my cousin, adding that anyone who upset Shirley would either be rewarded with an everlasting cold shoulder or a severe dressing down before being summarily dismissed from her life. Forever.

'It's interesting though, don't you think, how we tend to grow like them over time? I've already started demonstrating a few of *my* mother's tendencies.' A shiver ran down my spine at the mere contemplation of what my cousin was saying. I hurriedly tried to blot it out.

'Not a chance in my case. If I thought I had any of Shirley's unlikeable traits, I might just be tempted to end it all right now.' She laughed but in retrospect it was no laughing matter. In fact, I have, subsequently, lived to eat my words despite it taking quite a while for me to wake up and acknowledge my cousin's comments were absolutely spot on.

I'm not saying every person ends up displaying a lot, if not all, of their mother's characteristics and personality traits. Yet I think a great many do, whether they're aware of it or not. After all, when we spend an entire childhood being exposed to all the good, and not so good aspects that our mothers display, it's unlikely that none of them will ever rub off on us.

* * *

We were visiting the local shops after school one day when we encountered her.

'Shirley. It's really you. Goodness, it's been years. How lovely to see you. It's me, June.' 'Good heavens, I don't believe it, June Mitchell, how on earth did you recognise me?' Shirley patted her hair into place while critically eyeing her reflection in a shop window.

'Oh you haven't changed that much.' June laughed. 'I can still see you in your convent uniform.' I noticed she had a lovely twinkly kind of laugh that was quite unique. 'And who is this dear little girl?'

I looked up at June and immediately liked what I saw. A tall, very pretty lady with long, wild red hair, dressed in a flowing robe splattered with paint.

Shirley introduced me to June while apologising for my appearance. 'I've just picked her up from school, which may explain why she's looking such a mess. I assure you she didn't look like this when she left for school this morning.'

'Oh she looks gorgeous,' said June, bending down and planting a kiss on my forehead. I smiled my appreciation.

'I've got three of my own, now, would you believe? You must bring Ingrid around to play. Are you still doing the concert piano stuff? Or was it opera you were more into? I remember how good you were at both.'

'Yes I did study both,' Shirley wistfully answered, 'but … oh no, no time for all that anymore. Maybe when Ingrid's a bit older I may consider getting back into one or other field. But I'll probably have gone well off the boil by then. I don't even practice my scales as much as I should these days.'

'What, what do you do, at your house?' I was intrigued by June and wanted to know all about her.

'Ingrid, don't be so rude. This is grown-up time. Please don't interrupt.'

'No, don't worry, Shirley, she's just curious, which is a natural and lovely trait in a child. I'm an artist darling and I'm just on my way to the art shop to pick up some canvasses.' She gave me a beautiful smile. 'Maybe I'll paint your portrait one of these days? Would you like that?'

I nodded my agreement. 'Is that paint on your dress?'

'Oh June, I am sorry,' said an embarrassed Shirley, 'I quite forgot to ask about your art. How wonderful that you've kept it up. I'll look forward to seeing some of your work.'

They exchanged contact details and June invited us to tea the following week.

* * *

'What a tumbled down house they've got. I hope it's better on the inside.' Shirley was assessing June's home with distaste as she checked the address once more in the hope, no doubt, that we were at the wrong place.

Ringing the doorbell resulted in the arrival of three very excited, and according to Shirley, totally unruly children.

'Come, you can come, in,' said the smallest – a pretty little girl of about three sporting June's beautiful red hair.

'I'll open the gate for them.'

'No me, let me do it. It's my turn.'

'No it's not.'

The twin boys, who were a few years older than me, proceeded to fight one another for the privilege of opening the gate, when much to Shirley's relief, June arrived on the scene.

'She laughed her special *very* twinkly laugh. 'I'm so sorry Shirley. Do come in.'

She proceeded to ruffle the boys' hair and without reprimanding them at all, opened the gate herself.

If Shirley was disappointed at the outside of June's house she must have been totally devastated by the interior. It resembled a war zone that June's three children seemed to have full run of and run they did, in all directions, laughing, squealing with delight, and, *gasp*, jumping on furniture with gay abandon.

'Let's have our tea on the patio, outside my studio, shall we? It's so tranquil out there at this time of the day.'

Tea was also a very haphazard affair, compared to what I was used to, with children grabbing cups of tea as they were being poured and stuffing pieces of cake into their mouths before it could be offered to their guests.

'Tom, Tony, why don't you show Ingrid your tree house while I show Shirley some of my paintings?'

'It's *my* tee house,' claimed Abbey, the little three-year-old, 'I, I'll show … her.'

'She'll have to take off her shoes if she's going to climb up the tree ladder,' said Tom, looking disapprovingly at my feet. I noticed for the first time that all three children were barefoot.

Shirley quickly declined their invitation on my behalf. 'Oh no, no, no, maybe some other time, Ingrid isn't in any way dressed to climb trees. I definitely don't want her ruining the new dress she's wearing.'

It wasn't long after that we left. In fact it was just following Tony using a penknife to carve his initials on June's dining-room table.

'We've decided not to invest in expensive furniture until the children are older.' This explanation was hastily forthcoming from June at the sight of Shirley's disbelieving and very shell-shocked expression.

As we lived reasonably close to one another, June and her three children took to popping in, horror upon horrors, *uninvited.* They only did this successfully on one occasion, however, the first time, when as I recall they were not invited inside. No doubt the memory of the carving on June's dining-room table was still fresh in Shirley's mind. We had tea out of plastic mugs on the veranda.

On all subsequent visits we had to pretend we weren't at home until June and her brood went away.

'Good Lord,' exclaimed an indignant Shirley, by way of explanation for our strange behaviour, 'I can't understand why June chooses to dress herself and her children in rags and is incapable of teaching them how to behave. What on earth does she think they all look like? All I can say is that if they continue looking and behaving as they do, I can't imagine what will become of them all.'

As we never saw them again, after their last unsuccessful attempt to be welcomed to our home, history doesn't relate, but from my recollections they all seemed very happy.

I wished for a long, long time after their departure from my life that June had been able to paint my portrait.

* * *

I've been forced to recognise, but sadly only in recent years, that of all Shirley's unlikeable personality traits I'd identified I had adopted her penchant for judgment with the greatest of ease. When this finally dawned on me I also had to admit I'd actually lost count of how many friends and associates I'd dismissed from my own life over the years. This I'd managed without even being aware of how much damage I'd done to myself in the process.

I asked myself the same question over and over. 'How could I have grown so like Shirley, in the area of judgement in particular, without even noticing it was happening?' I can only think that I was so intent on being as unlike her as possible that it was inevitable that the opposite would occur. It's true. What we resist persists.

I became incredibly depressed when I eventually confronted myself about my highly judgmental personality. I wondered how I could ever make amends to all the undeserving recipients of it. It didn't take me long to work out that having dismissed so many from my life, but not before confronting them with all their wrongdoings, it was going to be difficult to make a comeback with any of them.

The best resolve I've managed to come up with, in an attempt to absolve myself from my crimes against humanity, is to ask everyone I've wronged, through prayer and meditation, to forgive me for judging them to be guilty of what they didn't do to me. As well as to endeavour, at the same time, to cease being judgmental going forward.

Old habits die hard, however, so I have to constantly and consciously remind myself of the perils of falling back into a judgmental state – even when I'm unconsciously getting on with my life. It is, after all, a state that was cultivated, little by little, over a large portion of my life. But, I'm glad to report, with eternal thanks to my strong feeling of connection with my Maker, it's getting easier to control, all the time.

* * *

'What are you planning to wear to Jackie's birthday party?'

'Nothing,' I replied from behind the book I was reading.

'What do you mean, nothing?' Shirley sat down with a deep sigh. 'It's only her 17th of course but I believe it's going to be a very grand affair so I sincerely hope you're not planning on just throwing on any old rag at the very last moment?'

I peered at her over the top of my book, wondering how long this disruption was going to last while also sensing it wasn't going to be a quickie as she continued to discuss the party.

'I'm quite prepared to buy you a new dress for the occasion, provided you'll allow me to help you select it, in place of one of your usual strange choices.' She lit a cigarette to celebrate her largess.

I admitted defeat by putting my book down and giving her the attention she was no doubt after.

'Well I wouldn't get too excited if I were you, I haven't been invited, so it's safe to say, as I did earlier, that I won't be wearing anything to the party.'

There was a deathly silence for a palpable second or so, followed by the lighting of another cigarette, despite the one already glowing in the ashtray next to her.

'I wonder if Thora knows that you haven't been invited,' Shirley mused. Thora was Jackie's mother and a close friend of Shirley's.

'I presume so. Claire's invitation appeared to come from Jackie's parents, as is the norm.'

'Claire's been invited, but not you?' Shirley looked shattered. 'When did Claire and Jackie become such good friends?' Shirley demanded to know with high indignation.

'They've always been friendly as far as I know.' I shrugged my shoulders as I picked up my book, hoping to escape from the conversation and continue where I'd left off.

'Well I'm willing to bet that Claire's mother hasn't known Thora half as long as I've known her.' Shirley got up and did an agitated route march around the lounge. 'Are you listening to me?'

I put my book down for the second time. 'Unfortunately I have no option, although you may have noticed that I'd rather be reading?'

Shirley paid no attention to what I had said. 'Never mind, there must be some mistake. I shall phone Thora and make sure you receive your invitation.'

'Oh no, please don't,' I begged. I couldn't believe she was going to humiliate me by interfering. Then again, why wouldn't I believe it?

'If you must know, Jackie and I are really not that friendly. We don't have the same interests. In fact we couldn't be more different. So if she doesn't want me at her party it's really fine with me – okay?'

'It's certainly not okay. She's just jealous of you, that's all. I've always sensed it. She just wishes she had your looks and personality and that even half the boys who are interested in you were interested in her.'

I had, unfortunately, been informed over the years that many people were jealous of me, or of her, or even of Bill, on occasion, depending on whatever resentment she was harbouring at the time. This, however, took the cake. I just couldn't believe the convoluted judgment Shirley had just made to explain why I hadn't been invited. But, just like all her judgments, it did set up an uncomfortable question mark in my brain. Was Jackie *really* jealous of me?

It wasn't the end of it, of course. I was forced to accept that Thora had eventually been badgered into sending me an invitation against Jackie's will, as it arrived long after everyone else had received theirs.

'I am not going to go,' I defiantly announced. 'I'll thank her for her invitation but tell her I have something else on that night.'

'You'll do nothing of the kind. After all the trouble I've gone to, to get you an invitation, you are definitely going. And what's more, by the time I'm finished selecting your dress and doing your hair, you are going to be the most sought after girl there by every boy present. Little Miss Jackie is going to find out that you are going to be the belle of her ball.'

On that note Shirley flounced out of the lounge in triumphant fashion.

I was eventually forced to go, but as you can imagine, under much duress. Jackie never even greeted me or spoke to me the entire night. Not because I was the belle of her ball, because I wasn't, but because I was there against her wishes. And mine. Although she didn't know that of course. I made sure that I was only present for the shortest possible time and, to hide my embarrassment at even being there at all, I kept to myself and spoke to as few people as possible. It was one of the worst nights of my life.

My attendance, by virtue of my engineered invitation, also impacted badly on Shirley and Thora's relationship, which sadly never recovered.

* * *

From the time we leave the protection of the real world that lives inside of us, courtesy of the inner spirit beauty of our birth, we automatically journey into the unreal outside world of our upbringing. This is a place that offers us the opportunity to learn lessons about why we shouldn't be there. Sound a bit weird? Well I guess so. Then again everything about the unreal outside world is indeed weird. This becomes very obvious when we compare it to the utter bliss of living in the inside world which is devoid of the need to judge or to be judged. But like all of us who have chosen the opportunity to become further enlightened, I've come to understand that experiencing judgment first hand and being aware of the consequences is very necessary – in order to avoid perpetuating it and the harm it causes.

When we first take up residence in the outside world and open ourselves up to the trauma of all manner of disturbing information and actions, it's not that surprising that we initially believe judgment of others is normal. In reality it's totally abnormal. The longer we live in the outside world, in an unenlightened state, the judging of others becomes as mechanical as eating and sleeping. Eventually we don't even stop to think about the judgments we pass, let alone think about why we are passing them in the first place, or how they may be affecting the recipients. Most important of all we appear to be totally unaware of how our judgments of others are adversely affecting us.

* * *

If I'd had any idea of the drama that was about to unfold, I would have advised Shirley I wouldn't be home for lunch.

'Well it looks as though it's just the two of us. Your father has decided to eat at the Yacht Club with David. They've decided to sail again this afternoon. Heaven knows why, it looks pretty grey and threatening out there.' Shirley made this observation while looking out the window and viewing the ocean from a fair distance. She also downed the last drop of her pre-lunch sherry.

I sat down and abstractedly scanned the first page of the supplement to the Sunday paper. 'What about Connie? She's coming isn't she? She always comes to lunch on Sundays. Aren't we going to wait for her?' I posed the questions in the hope that it wasn't just going to be Shirley and me staggering our way through lunch on our own.

'Past tense,' Shirley announced, folding her arms protectively over her chest.

'Why, has she died or something?' Connie had been coming to Sunday lunch for as long as I could remember.

'She might just as well as far as I'm concerned.' She then did something quite unusual. She poured another sherry despite normally restricting herself to just one before meals.

'Why? What's happened?' I decided I might as well join the party and poured myself a glass of the wine that had been opened for lunch.

'She had the cheek to tell me that she wouldn't be able to come today because she's having her new best friend, Ellen, *and* Ellen's daughter, to lunch.' Shirley took a bigger sip than usual from her sherry glass.

'Yes, so … what's wrong with that?' I was hoping my glass of wine would help me to make sense of what had gone down between the two of them.

'What's wrong with that?' Shirley was furious. 'I'll tell you what's wrong with that. As you correctly stated earlier, Connie always comes *here* for Sunday lunch. And has been for goodness knows how long. But has she ever invited me to have lunch at her home on a Sunday?'

'I don't know. Has she? Hasn't she?' I wished I'd never asked if Connie was coming to lunch. In retrospect I would've done better to have continued my involvement with the supplement I'd been reading.

'Of course not. She, just like everyone else, takes me and my hospitality totally for granted. Until now of course. Now that she's become so friendly with *Ellen*, I am no longer of any use to her.' She sniffed. It was beginning to alarm me how Shirley was most uncharacteristically tucking into the sherry.

'Look Mum, let's be honest here, Connie comes to Sunday lunch when it suits *you*. You recall I hope that you do on occasion go elsewhere on a Sunday? On those Sundays she's not invited.'

'Yes, well of course not we're not joined at the hip you know. But, well, I've always felt so sorry for her, since Howard's untimely death, that I've, I've always tried to have her over as often as possible and … and this is the way she repays me.'

Shirley stood up. I'd hoped it was in order to retrieve lunch from the kitchen, but no doubt the effects of the sherry were beginning to hit home as she abruptly sat down again. 'Are you okay? You've been downing that sherry like there's no tomorrow. Shall I get you a glass of water?

She burst into tears. 'I'm so tired of being so kind to people and having them treat me so badly. What have I ever done to deserve such treatment from Connie?'

I really didn't want to answer that question. Truthfully or untruthfully. Shirley was after all highly judgmental. The closer she got to people, she mistakenly assumed she had earned the right to judge them in matters that were none of her business. I knew that Connie had often come under the whip for doing things Shirley considered to be unwise or unacceptable. I wondered if Connie wasn't perhaps suffering from an overdose of Shirley's judgments and had decided to take a sabbatical from the Sunday lunch experience.

'I'm going to get a jug of water from the kitchen, so just hang in there, I won't be long.' When I returned, I found Shirley, although slightly more composed, still dabbing at her eyes with a tissue.

'Oh come on Mum, I know Connie's very fond of you, despite your spats over the years. I'm willing to bet this whole thing with Ellen is just a storm in a teacup.'

I took another gulp of wine quickly followed by a gulp of water, realising that I too had uncharacteristically allowed all the unhappiness over Connie to lead to a second glass. I looked forward to eating something soon. After all I needed to swat for an exam later and at this rate I could find myself having an afternoon nap instead. Shirley, however, put paid to the thought of food by starting to cry all over again. I put it down to the sherry.

As I have previously mentioned, we weren't a demonstrative family, so instead of throwing my arms around her and drying her tears, I patted her on the shoulder and handed her another tissue.

'I bet the next time we all sit down for Sunday lunch, Connie will be here too.'

'No, she won't,' she sobbed, 'I told her I never want to see her again as long as I live and that she is under no circumstance to ever contact me again.'

And that was that. I never saw Connie again at a Sunday lunch. Or anywhere else for that matter.

* * *

Each one of us is represented by a tiny fragment of love within our Maker's giant hologram of love. So it's understandable that when we judge others with the intention of hurting them that we are not only hurting ourselves but judging ourselves as well. And self-judgment is far more detrimental to us than being judged by others. When others judge us there is no need to buy into the judgments at all because quite simply, they are not real.

What's real is that we are perfectly beautiful eternal spirits clothed in human form to experience and grow from our knowledge of life on Planet Earth. These experiences enable us to return to the place from which we originally come as greatly enlightened beautiful beings. We cannot therefore ever be judged to be imperfect. We are the only ones who can do that to ourselves, by choosing to accept the harmful judgments of others, and thereby making those judgments real. The same applies when the receiver of *our* judgments believes they are real and can harm *them.*

In reality, because we are not separate from one another but all part of the whole universal love of our Maker, the giver of the judgment also becomes the receiver of it. Therefore, the more we judge others simply increases our judgment of ourselves.

Over time we find ourselves the unhappy recipients of great multitudes of judgments that start to weigh very heavily on our shoulders and our hearts.

The unreal beliefs that we are imperfect, negative beings as opposed to the perfect, positive beings our Maker created us to be, start to consume us. This makes us incredibly unhappy, dissatisfied and unfulfilled as we struggle to experience everything that we consider to be desirable and satisfying. That, in turn, means we are judging ourselves unworthy of the love, joy, fun, freedom, security, prosperity, fulfilment, peace and satisfaction that is ours to enjoy.

* * *

'Can you tell me the reasons why you were specifically drawn to *this* job, Ingrid?' Phyllis smiled at me encouragingly as she sat back in her large executive chair to hear what my ambitions were for the company.

She was a friend of Shirley's who held the high position of head of marketing, answerable only to the founder and CEO and had been asked by Shirley to interview little ole me for a job as her PA. Poor Phyllis had probably been as reluctant as I was to have been propelled into the interview.

'To be honest Phyllis, I can't supply you with even one reason.' I pulled a face that I hoped she'd recognise as an upfront apology for my presence on the other side of her desk. She put her head back and laughed. 'Not even one?'

'Personally, I think I'd be way out of my depth as your PA, although I'm sure the remuneration I believe you're offering could turn me into a fast busker.' It was my turn to laugh.

'And why do you think you're not really up to it?' She'd regained her composure and was smiling at me like a benevolent aunt – which she was, of course, but not of the blood variety.

'Well firstly, I'm not really PA material. My true talent lies somewhere on the creative side of the spectrum. But I haven't yet decided exactly where.' I lifted my hands and arms in the air to demonstrate my lack of clarity.

'Ah yes, pity you didn't follow through with your interest in speech and drama – I always felt you had a definite gift for that. What exactly did you do overseas?'

'Now, now Phyllis you don't want me to lower the tone of this meeting by encouraging me to go into detail about that do you?' I winked at her and she laughed once more.

'You're incorrigible ... but Shirley has already informed me that you also managed to hold down a few top marketing jobs while you were abroad?'

'If you consider handing out brochures on the BMW stand at the London Motor Show, dressed in Bavarian Costume, as marketing, then she would be correct.'

'Oh Ingrid,' she chuckled and shook her head at the same time, 'Tell me what else you got up to? Go on, I'm a big girl, l can take it.' This time we both laughed.

'Well, a few months after I called off the wedding, which I'm sure you've heard all about, a friend of mine who was trying to set up a business in Europe asked me if I'd like to join him on, would you believe, a marketing trip to the South of France.' Phyllis nodded, presumably indicating her knowledge of the breakup with Grant as well as her approval of a trip to the South of France. 'While we were there I met a friend of his, a Brit who runs a Villa Rental Company out of Saint Tropez. He offered me a job there for the summer, as a Villa representative.'

'How wonderful, that must've been great fun?' Phyllis clasped her hands with enthusiasm.

'It was, it's always great to be paid, albeit not a great deal, to go to the beach every day and occasionally sort out the odd villa problem. Or perhaps even make a restaurant booking or two for clients. But, once again, I can positively assure you it wasn't a conventional marketing job either, by any stretch of the imagination.' 'Ah well my dear, your mother thinks so highly of you I'm sure she'd applaud anything you do.' She leaned over the desk and warmly squeezed my hands.

I was almost dumbstruck by her comment but managed a reply accompanied by a half laugh. 'Yes of course, anything.' Well "stone the crows" I thought to myself. Shirley was proving to be a far better marketer than I'd ever be. She was successfully promoting me while having no faith in "Brand Ingrid" whatsoever.

'If I don't offer you this job, what do you think you'll do?' Phyllis looked at me in a concerned sort of way. 'Well, between you and me, Bill, unbeknown to Shirley, has already enrolled me at a business college to get a piece of paper I can fall back on if I change my mind and decide to become a PA after all. Let's see what happens?'

'Let's do that,' said the pragmatic Phyllis. 'If you still need a job after you've completed the course, I'll do all in my power to create one for you here, in line with your experience.'

* * *

'I can't believe Phyllis didn't offer you the position.'

Shirley could hardly wait to quiz me on the outcome of the interview and was bitterly disappointed when I'd moved my index finger across my neck to indicate the death of the job.

'I'm seriously beginning to believe that she had no intention of …'

I cut her off in mid rant. 'Oh come on, she's a big deal. She needs a highly experienced PA to organise her life. And as you keep reminding me, I can't even organise my own life.'

I walked past her into the kitchen and opened the fridge to see what was cooking – it was always my favourite refuge when I sensed Shirley was on one of her missions. But she followed me of course. 'That's only because you've never applied yourself. She could have at least given you a trial period to prove your worth. I feel completely let down by Phyllis. I've never asked her for anything in my entire life … and I can assure you, I never, ever will, ever again.'

'For goodness sake, stop judging her so harshly and banging on about it … can I perhaps interest you in a nice piece of cold chicken and a glass of white wine instead?' It was a lame attempt to change the subject and needless to say, it didn't work.'

'In fact I can't imagine myself ever speaking to her again.' Shirley continued to doggedly pursue the topic and emphasised her comment by hitting the kitchen table with a clenched fist.

So I guess it won't come as a great surprise to find out that, sadly, she never did speak to her again.

* * *

As a matter of interest, next time you catch yourself starting to judge another it might be worth remembering the injustice you are about to inflict on yourself. It may just prevent you from completing the judgment and thereby save you from receiving it straight back.

Just as cigarette smokers make their once pink lungs darker and darker with every additional cigarette they smoke, until their lungs become pitch black with continual nicotine staining, so it is with all the dark judgements with which we fill up our once pure bodies.

As soon as smokers stop smoking their lungs begin to repair and revert over time to their original healthy colour – faster and faster with every cigarette they don't smoke.

When we stop judging others, and thereby ourselves, an equally pleasant transformation occurs in our beings. The pain, fear, bitterness, unhappiness, dissatisfaction and heaviness we have been carrying around starts to lift, making room for more and more love, fun, joy, security, fulfilment, happiness, satisfaction, peace and prosperity.

# Chapter 13

# Married to my Mother

After the unhappy events of the cancelled wedding, I remained in the UK for a while, followed by another eight months or more in France before returning for some reason to South Africa. In retrospect, it might well have had something to do with lack of money – actually now that I think about it I'm almost certain it did. I had worked intermittently at part time jobs in both of the aforementioned countries but of course never earned a great deal. Bill, however, always came to the party by sending me money whenever I ran out. That was until shortly before my return, when he warned that his generosity wasn't going to last forever and that the best solution was for me was to come home and resume my studies or get a job.

* * *

My homecoming was chilly to say the least even though it was a hot and sticky KwaZulu-Natal summer. Bill seemed pre-occupied with "other things" and Shirley was still smarting at the fact that I had given up a chance of living the beautiful life of "They".

'Why you gave up everything to go tripping around Europe with no plan in mind for your future is beyond me. You clearly have no ambition whatsoever.'

I had to admit, *to myself*, that my life was not perfect by any stretch of the imagination. I vowed I would try harder from that moment on to be more like the person Shirley needed me to be.

After embarking on a course at a business college, in order to acquire some rudimentary office skills, I counted myself fortunate to get a job as a lowly paid PA. Lucky for me my boss was a really super guy who bravely put up with what I am sure was a pretty mediocre job performance on my part. I offset the daily grind by joining a theatre group at the same time. This resulted in work by day and fun times by night as the group rehearsed and partied in equal measure. When I presented my long-suffering boss with comps to attend the play, I think he finally realised why I wasn't ideal PA material and also why I needed several cups of black coffee every morning.

It was also at that stage of my precarious life that I met another man. Shirley approved of him immediately. He wasn't the son of her soul mate but he did tick most of the other boxes and was therefore a close second. In fact, let's be honest, she had a bigger than normal soft spot for him and I believe she grew to love him like the son she never had.

It didn't dawn on me immediately but I did subsequently come to realise that they got on so well because they were so much alike. In retrospect, and because of their similarities, I believe my post wedding relationship with my husband must have unconsciously felt like slipping into a pair of well-worn slippers.

The strange thing was that despite her approval and enthusiasm for him from the word go, I rather fancied him myself. What I saw in the beginning was a kind, affectionate and generous person with whom I shared the same sense of humour. This translated into a fun, laughter-filled relationship. He was also well-read and interested in a wide range of subjects so we could talk about practically everything under the sun. I also found him very attractive and he treated me like a princess. So, most things considered, it was no surprise we decided to get married.

* * *

Unfortunately, however, due to a few other things that had come to light, I began to think, shortly before the wedding, that my future husband was perhaps not quite the ideal choice after-all.

I was always aware that he enjoyed more than "a" drink, and that on some occasions he could unnecessarily overdo it. But … well, I rationalised that he didn't drink every day so how bad was it if he let his hair down now and then? As his consumption began to be more in evidence prior to our marriage, my initial assessment however started to change.

Something else that occupied my pre-marital thoughts even more than his drinking was our sex life. Although it had never been exceptional, I believed the affection we had for one another was warm and special. And as affection was something I craved more than anything else I naively believed that we would, in time, be able to channel it into a good sexual relationship. But in the run up to the wedding I couldn't help noticing that intimate displays of affection instigated by my husband-to-be were becoming more and more sporadic while his encounters with alcohol never waned.

I had of course discussed both conditions with him on several occasions. His plausible response was always the same. He was under a lot of stress and pressure as he was after all studying for the last leg of a degree that had eluded him for some time, while holding down a fulltime job. Once we were married, he'd said, all would be well and wonderful as he would have so much more time to devote to making me happy. He also promised faithfully to curb his alcohol intake too.

Nevertheless, a strong feeling of "deja vu" had crept over me making me feel very uncomfortable indeed. Was I destined to continue meeting men, deciding to marry them, and then running for the hills shortly before the wedding took place? There was, however, one thing of which I was certain. Shirley would not survive another wedding cancellation. So this time, despite warning signs that all was not one hundred per cent well in Camelot, plans for the big event went ahead, as did the event itself.

Just a week before the wedding I contracted a bad dose of flu. Probably with hindsight it was a nudge from the Universe that this attempt at a wedding was going to be as disastrous as the first. With that in mind the flu progressed to bronchitis and in turn to a course of strong antibiotics which my doctor prescribed to get me fit for my "big day".

Miraculously, when the day dawned, I'd made the orchestrated recovery. 'You look remarkably well,' Shirley had said, packing a little more concealer under my eyes while she helped me to get ready. 'Nobody would say you've been so sick.' I had to finish the course of antibiotics, however, and that's where the problem came in. They didn't mix too well with the whisky Bill gave me to steady my nerves before leaving for the church. Or with the wine I consumed at the reception. I drank far too much of it and was as sick as a dog at the hotel where we spent our first night as "newly-weds".

I didn't feel that much better the next day either and our planned trip to the mountains had to be put on hold because I was just too ill to travel.

* * *

Bill had opened the front door with a chuckle and a quizzical smile.

'Brought her back already, have you?'

As our new apartment didn't boast air-con, to cope with the intense summer humidity my husband suggested we spend our second night at my parents' home so I could recover in comfort. It was a considerate suggestion, of course, but as we both ended up in separate beds for the second night in a row, I couldn't help thinking that it was an unusual way to start a marriage, even if I wasn't feeling that well.

As we set off the next day on our second attempt to reach our honeymoon destination, I was feeling a whole lot better. My husband unfortunately took a turn for the worse. It was in fact such a bad turn that it remained part of our married life for the entire duration of it.

* * *

'You do know you're a nymphomaniac don't you?' I was completely gob-smacked to hear this. 'Why can't you just take this opportunity to relax and get better?' He got up abruptly, picked up his pillow and moved from the bed to the couch.

I felt totally crushed. A deep pain that started in the region of my heart finally engulfed my very being as I felt a million tears of rejection well up inside me. Instead of letting them run free in order to purge myself of their unwanted presence, accumulated over a lifetime of feeling starved of affection, I turned my face to the wall. And only let the few I couldn't control to dampen my unseen cheeks.

We'd been away for almost a week and so far my husband hadn't made so much as a move to even hold my hand. Even kissing and cuddling initiated by me had suddenly become a decided no-no. It was so bad that every time my foot so much as accidently brushed up against his in bed, he'd quickly move away. I wasn't sure what the hell was going on. I mentioned previously that the physical side of our relationship never sparkled like the 5th November but to find that our usual displays of affection had also disappeared from our lives was something I just couldn't get my head around. As he refused to discuss the matter, I chose to believe that something that was going to remain unknown to me had upset him. I also naively believed that things would suddenly revert to our pre-marital relationship.

As it turned out, however, my belief wasn't strong enough and just hoping the situation would correct itself was simply never going to be enough.

It became obvious, from our so called "honeymoon" onwards, that my husband wasn't really into intimacy at all. I began to feel that he'd previously only been pretending to be.

The situation was intolerable in as much as it re-ignited my abandonment complex exponentially. Forget about sinking into a big black hole of despair, it felt more like a crater. What was happening was completely at odds with what I'd experienced in other intimate relationships and what I'd grown up to believe was important to men.

* * *

The lesson I learned, or thought I'd learned, about the needs of men happened the same year as the arrival of my first monthly period, the death of my grandmother and the only light in a very dark tunnel, coming first in my class. My twelfth year. A year when I also discovered, by chance, that Bill, who always enjoyed female company, was having an affair. Not the first it turned out and not the last.

* * *

'Don't you *ever* hurt my mother.' It was probably the only time in my life that I'd jumped to Shirley's defence.

'Look Ingy, I know what you saw upset you darling, but, well I, I was just kissing Aunty Patsy happy birthday. That's all.'

'It's not her birthday and she's not my aunt. She's been hanging around here ever since we met her and that old mother of hers in the midlands at Easter, and now I know why. She's just been pretending to be Mummy's friend. Tell her never to come back here, ever again.'

After my initial outburst we had sat down to have, what Bill termed, a "grown-up" conversation.

'I think it's important we sort this out. You're not an adult yet, of course … but, well, you've asked me specifically to never hurt your mother, and I want to reassure you I never will. But you also have to play your part and never hurt her either …"

'What do you mean?'

'You must promise me you'll never discuss this uh, Patsy incident, with your mother.' I could see he was uncomfortable by the way he moved about in his chair.'

'Why? So you can carry on kissing Patsy without her knowing?'

'You have to understand why it happened.'

'I think I know *why.*' I defiantly folded my arms. After all I knew all about sex – my school friend Elaine and I had discussed it at length. Certainly the way Bill had been kissing Patsy wasn't in a happy birthday kind of way.

'You may think you know why, but when you're a grown up you'll look back on what I'm going to say … and probably understand it a whole lot better.'

'Try me.' I had no intention of making the situation easy on him. I could hear the challenging tone in my voice ringing in my ears.

Bill, however, tried to be as understanding as possible. 'Well, the truth is, your mother isn't a particularly, well let's just say, she's not a very affectionate person. He nervously tapped the top of his thighs with both hands. She doesn't really enjoy giving or receiving affection. It's just not her thing.' He then rubbed the side of his nose with his index finger.

'So?' I fixed him with what I hoped was a fierce stare.

'So, not wanting to, to make her feel uncomfortable about that I, well I choose instead to show my affection to other people.' This time he rubbed his chin.

'People like Patsy, I suppose?'

He nodded while gently chewing on the inside of his cheek.

'And what about sex? Do you have sex with her too?'

'Oh my God.' He lifted his head and looked heavenward. 'What do *you know* about sex?' He clearly hadn't banked on the conversation going in that direction.

'I know people don't only have sex to have babies. Elaine's mother told her *everything* – and she's told me.'

'Well then,' said Bill, abruptly getting to his feet, 'in that case you should also know that your mother doesn't enjoy sex either.'

With that parting shot he walked out of the room.

I was totally shocked to hear this. Elaine and I thought *everyone* enjoyed sex. In fact up until then I believed it was what everybody mostly lived for. I immediately vowed in my innocent half child, half adult way that my husband, whoever he might turn out to be, would never have to accuse me of not being affectionate and not wanting to have sex with him. Little did I know then that the man I'd choose to be my husband would, soon after our marriage, begin to demonstrate his highly critical side and confirm his lack of interest in sex. And that they would prove to be the two most important characteristics he and Shirley had in common.

* * *

'Surely you know we can't carry on like this. Don't you want to, to at least *try* to make things work?' I asked this long overdue question as I agitatedly flipped through a magazine while my husband intently watched a rugby match on TV. Yet even as the words left my mouth, I regretted bringing it up in the middle of the game.

He snapped the top off another bottle of beer. When he replied it was as a man living in total denial would do. 'There you go again, spoiling everything.'

'How can I spoil a situation that's already spoilt, and has been, virtually since we got married. If not before.'

'Come on boy, come on, go, go, go. Now man, nowww. *Dammit*, when're they going to drop this guy, he never knows when to pass the bloody ball.'

He'd jumped to his feet, shouting encouragement during the player's run for the try line but now flopped back onto the couch in utter disappointment.

I took a sip of wine from my glass, feeling relieved that my comment of earlier wasn't going to be blamed for the wing's lack of ability to score or pass the ball.

It was half time. He leaned back and looked up at the ceiling. 'We were getting on just fine, thanks to you not mentioning it for nearly a month.'

'Oh were we? That's nice to know.'

He glared at me. 'Yes we were, and I can do without your sarcasm. There are other things in life besides sex in case you haven't noticed.'

The absence of intimacy in our lives was no doubt disturbing but what was even more upsetting was the disappearance of the affection that went with it. In fact it was destroying me a little bit more each day. This resulted in me visiting my GP on a regular basis and presenting with an assortment of ills like headaches, head colds and sinus problems as well as the most recent malady, a recurring dose of debilitating flu. All of this ultimately resulted in my doctor deciding to examine my newly-married lifestyle with many probing questions. It was this investigation that inevitably involved my husband, with unhappy consequences.

* * *

He was waiting for me in the lounge of our apartment on the day it all came to a head and he was more than a little upset.

'So tell me, did you get a kick out of discussing our private life with *your doctor?*' He glared at me with resentment as I gingerly took a seat on the couch opposite him.

'Oh crumbs,' I muttered, as much to myself as to him as I suddenly realised what was going down.

'I, I'm sorry, I didn't know he was going to … did he contact you?'

'Of course he did. What the hell possessed you to discuss "us" with him?'

'It … well … it's just that I've been sick a lot lately and he, well, he wanted to know why.' I rubbed my clammy palms on the sides of my jeans.

'And you told him it's because I don't make love to you often enough, is that right?' He stood up, looked out the window and then sat down again. The view presumably didn't offer him the inspiration he was hoping for.

'No, well … he asked me if everything was okay between us, and, and that's when I admitted it wasn't.'

'And you expect me to believe that? I bet you couldn't wait to complain about the so-called, lack, of what interests you most, sex.'

I screamed in retaliation. 'How many times must I tell you that I can do without sex but I can't handle the new distant you. There's … there's no affection in our lives anymore.'

I might just as well have said nothing. He continued his rant based on *his belief* of how things were between us. 'I can just imagine what you told him and why he couldn't wait to phone me to ask me to come and see him about your "ill-health".' Hell, I've never driven as fast in my life – only to find out that there's nothing wrong with you, except perhaps for the sickness in your head.' He went into the kitchen and returned with a newly-opened bottle of beer. 'Jesus. He had the nerve to tell me he couldn't lower your libido, which, by the way, he thinks is quite normal … and that's only because he doesn't really know what a nympho you are.'

I closed my eyes in an obviously vain attempt to block out some of the pain of his words as he took a swig from his bottle. 'But this is the best. He also told me he's confident he can increase *mine* with treatment. Treatment? Both of you are insane. I'm not going to have any treatment or take drugs for a condition that I don't have.'

'I'm sorry but … but I don't know anything about that. He, he never discussed it with me.' I felt tearful and hugged a cushion for comfort.

'Oh, I'm sure he didn't.' With every swig of beer he took he was becoming increasingly sarcastic too.

'Well I've told him, and you can tell him again next time you see him for one of your cozy little chats that there's nothing wrong with my sex drive.' He was shouting at this point. 'It's perfectly normal, but it just can't match the demands of a sex addict like you.' He jumped to his feet, quickly crossed the floor to the front door, opened it and slammed it behind him as he left.

Once I was alone, I began to cry uncontrollably. I didn't know what to do about everything. I felt utterly helpless and hopeless. We'd been married for just a few months and the problems we were experiencing seemed insurmountable. Sex had always guaranteed affection in my *fucked-up* world. But now that there was none in our married life there was definitely no demonstrations of love and affection either. There was a whole lot of drinking though. But just by one of us.

* * *

'Where the hell did you buy your bloody license,' he slurred, 'Jeeesus. Lemme out of this car before you kill us.' Getting out at the next stop street he exchanged the passenger seat for a seat on the pavement, from where he continued to berate me.

This was the first in what became a fairly normal occurrence when I was forced to drive us home from social events. If I forgot to apply the child locks to the doors it was something that was almost guaranteed. What's more, it always resulted in me having to circle the block a few times before I could coerce him back into the car without holding up the traffic behind me.

I'd got used to driving us when he was too drunk to do so but I could never get used to being verbally abused at the same time mostly for my purported lack of driving skills. I eventually worked out, however, that it had nothing to do with my driving. It had, instead, everything to do with his desire to make me feel as inadequate as he himself no doubt felt – in situations where he was incapable of getting behind the wheel. All in all I was now living with a stranger compared to the man I'd met on my return to South Africa.

* * *

The overwhelming fear I'd felt at being abandoned in the early years of my marriage initially resulted in me becoming extremely withdrawn. It was the same sort of feeling I experienced when I had to leave my grandmother to go and live with my parents. I couldn't think rationally anymore. I felt like a child again, guilty of all the criticisms levelled against me without fully understanding why I'd never been criticised like this before we got married.

I lost my confidence completely and could only assume that I was the cause of his rejection of me. I had surely become the ugliest creature on the planet. Not for the first time in my life I was dwelling on outer beauty as being one of the main ingredients in successful relationships. Why else was I suffering like this? How could my marriage, which I had always thought would be one of the closest unions I'd ever experience, due to my childhood commitment to always please my husband, have transformed my life into a total torment?

During this period I also participated in visits to many marriage guidance counsellors and a sex therapist with my husband in order to "save our marriage". He continued to believe, despite the fact we weren't having *any* sexual relations by that stage, that I was highly over-sexed while he himself had a perfectly normal appetite for it. Having discounted the opinion of my doctor, in the very early stages of our marriage, he was now hoping for reassurance regarding the normalcy of his libido from other experts in their field. This of course failed to happen.

'If you're not particularly interested in sex, do you mind me asking why you chose to marry a sexy girl?' This totally unexpected, jaw dropping view was posed by the first marriage counsellor we consulted. He looked uncomfortable at the question so chose to answer it with a shrug of his shoulders. I on the other hand was so ecstatic to hear that somebody, albeit a middle-aged woman with grey hair and glasses, thought I was sexy I nearly kissed her with relief and gratitude. In fact I became so emboldened by her first comment in this regard, but a view that she continued to share with us throughout our visits with her, that it gave me the courage to embark on an extra marital affair.

The affair didn't come about because I'd fallen madly in love with the other person but in order to reassure myself that I was still attractive to members of the opposite sex. Most important of all to feel warmth and affection again.

Bearing in mind, however, that my self-esteem had taken such a giant knock, it took me a long time to pick up the pieces and reconstruct myself. Due to my abandonment issues, the best place to perform this reconstruction seemed, from my jaundiced perspective at the time, to be from within the safety and false security of my marriage.

At that juncture I was in no way strong enough to leave my husband, and as a result risk another serious relationship that could also potentially end in abuse and abandonment. The first liaison was short lived but led to another longer lasting one as my confidence gradually returned and I began telling myself that I was leading a happy life. The sadness deep inside me unfortunately remained like a constant dull ache, even though I'd tried to bury it. Over time though, I did begin to believe, on the surface anyway, my own lie.

* * *

I was working as a copywriter in the advertising industry which, at the time, boasted a party culture of note – within the agencies themselves and within all associated arms of it too. Extra-marital affairs were also considered to be a perfectly normal by-product of the party culture. So, in a sick kind of way, I was starting to fit into my new life perfectly.

It may appear to have been a very shallow way of living and I'm certainly not in any way suggesting it wasn't. But for someone who was just coming out of a nightmare of self-doubt about practically everything, my outward appeal in particular, it seemed to be the perfect environment to get myself back on track. Without any strings attached. Or so I initially thought.

My husband in fact was the first to benefit from my elicit relationships. I had come to the realisation that he was never going to revert to the person he'd been when we first met, but more importantly that I no longer needed him to validate my appeal. The pressure I'd previously put on him to try and address our problems, ceased. In this more relaxed atmosphere, we were able to get along far better. In fact, even our ability to laugh and talk about most things, except ourselves of course, returned.

What followed was a perfectly plastic private and social life filled with entertaining, and being entertained, partying and holidaying both locally and overseas with an assortment of friends and acquaintances and even on our own. He travelled overseas a lot in connection with his job so when it came to holidays, he preferred local activities like fishing and windsurfing. I, on the other hand, loved everything international holiday travel offered. So we were able to successfully compromise in that area of our lives by doing both.

Even Shirley, who never *really* got her head around what I did for a living, despite my ongoing explanations to try and educate her on the subject, nevertheless applauded my success on the work front. This was particularly the case when she started to witness the material gains that it brought into my life. She was equally impressed with the state of my marriage, which she also considered very successful. As far as Shirley was concerned I was at last living the beautiful life of "They". Or close to it anyway. You must remember that when it came to "They" Shirley attributed exceptionally high standards.

I remember her relaying an incident to me at the time that perfectly illustrated her idea of what married bliss was all about. 'Jean,' she said, referring to a friend of hers, 'had the audacity to suggest to me the other day that you should have had children by now.'

'Good grief,' I said, 'if you lived the life that Ingrid and her husband lead, the last thing you'd want to do is spoil it with children.'

I didn't tell her of course, but I had by that time decided that I definitely wanted children. I foolishly began to hope that I would be able to meet Mr Right while still married to Mr Wrong – not only for the purpose of having children, but also in order to experience happiness ever after. But just who the *hell* was I kidding? Only myself as it turned out. When I finally did meet who I thought was Mr Right, the ridiculous notion I had of him scooping me up in his manly arms and taking me away to a life of eternal bliss, love and contentment proved to be a total myth.

* * *

When I told him in a moment of madness, but truth, that I couldn't bear to go on living without him by my side *all the time* and as such had decided to divorce my husband so that he and I could be together forever, I opened myself up for yet another severe dose of emotional abandonment.

It turned out in fact that he wasn't totally unhappy with the status quo. Although he wasn't averse to me leaving my husband he definitely wasn't inclined to officially leave his wife with whom he shared business interests of a substantial financial nature.

'No … it won't work … it's impossible, we've just got far too much to lose if I leave her. As long as she and I continue to live under a veneer of respectability she'll be happy … and we can be too … even more than we already are.' He suddenly started to kiss me, no doubt in preparation for the more important things on his mind. I abruptly pulled away. 'Did you just say "We've" got far too much to lose?' He poured himself another glass of wine from the bottle we'd been sharing over lunch at our little hide-away before he delivered his measured response.

'Yes, … if you leave *him*, we won't have to pussy-foot around anymore – we can start doing more together – local and overseas trips – whatever we want … just … just as long I don't upset the financial apple cart with *her*, by never *ever* even hinting at a divorce. That way I'll be able to continue to spoil you to my heart's content … and you know how I love spoiling you, don't you?' He lovingly stroked my arm. ' We can even …

'I cut him off in mid-sentence. 'What!?' I vividly remember throwing my glass of wine against the wall in a rage. 'Are you suggesting that if I leave my husband for you that I can officially become your bloody mistress?' I was screaming and crying all at the same time. I felt helpless and devastated … alone and disillusioned.

There were many more incidents like that of course. It was so hard to even contemplate breaking away. Not knowing anything about true love at that stage of my existence I continued to feel life without him would be like a living death. He was my daily love drug that I found so hard to do without – whether he was with me in person or just talking to me on the phone.

So making up and breaking up became the order of the day. But rather than cover this page in *all the schmaltz* I felt for him, and how he broke my heart in ten million pieces, let me just say this instead. All things being considered he eventually left me with no option but to walk away. Albeit on very unsteady legs. The alternative was to become further embroiled in yet another relationship that I knew in my heart of hearts was never likely to improve and I wasn't strong enough for that.

If I was to try and describe how I felt about our final parting, I'd say it was like a slow burn that started in some small place inside of me … and eventually occupied all of me. No, no, not really. Let's be real here. The pain was much worse than that … however … well that's just the way it was destined to be.

Yet not before our secret relationship became a secret no more.

* * *

My husband was dressed for work, holding a coffee mug in an unsteady hand. He was also furious. I, on the other hand, was completely taken aback to have found his car parked in the driveway and him standing in the hallway. My heart was beating like a kettle drum. I felt like a schoolgirl who had been caught out playing truant.

'Well that's nice. I come home from an overseas trip a day early and find you're not even here. You spend the whole night away and nobody has a clue where you are. Not even the maid. Fortunately she fed the dogs. You don't seem to care about them anymore either?'

I immediately felt defensive when being accused of neglecting my pets.

It was telling that I considered that more important than being accused of not being at home for him. 'She's been told, *by me*, to feed the dogs if I'm not here.'

'Oh,' he said seizing on what he considered to be an admission of my guilt, 'so you're not here that often then?'

'I didn't say that, you did.' I wasn't going to join in a "you said, no I said" debate. 'Can we discuss this tonight, I need to shower and change or I'm going to be late for work.'

He wasn't going to let me off the hook that easily. He grabbed my arm as I tried to walk past. 'If I find out you're having an affair, I swear, I'll kill you both.'

That's when I finally snapped. I abruptly pulled my arm out of his grip as my anger over-flowed. 'Oh for God's sake, stop being so pathetic and melodramatic. When you decide to start treating me like a wife and … and acting like, like a proper husband, that's when you can start telling me I can't sleep with anyone else.'

The blood drained from his face. I think he'd suppressed everything to such an extent that this was his first forced awareness that our marriage had become a total charade. I wanted to take back my hateful words almost immediately after uttering them but it was too late for that, of course. For the first time in ages I allowed myself to feel a deep sadness for him, myself and our situation. He turned on his heels and left without another word. In line with the way we handled all our marital problems, by sweeping them under the carpet, we never spoke about the incident ever again.

* * *

'You'll never guess where I've been?'

She was a PA in the client service department of the advertising agency where I was working at the time and she was extremely excited to impart her news as she entered my office and sat down opposite me.

'Surprise me,' I said with a smile. And she did.

'I've been eating Sushi and other Japanese delights with your husband. He's doing business with Peter, my fiancé, and kindly invited both of us to lunch.

'Oh, that's nice,' I said as I took a sip of water from my bottle. It was a coincidence, of course, that her fiancé knew my husband but I wondered what all the excitement was about.

'You are soooo lucky. He is such an awesome guy, isn't he?' She positively sparkled at her discovery. I smiled and nodded weakly. 'The first thing he did was to ask me all about myself. When I told him I worked here he immediately wanted to know if I knew you.'

'Oh right.' *Of course he had*, I thought to myself. He'd been brought up to do that in order to make new acquaintances feel at ease – and often chastised me for not being more interested in enquiring about the ins and outs of the lives of others we met in social gatherings.

'Wow, is that guy crazy about you or what?' She positively beamed with enthusiasm. 'As soon as I said, of course I know you, his eyes just lit up with love and he took out his wallet to show us all the photos of you he carries around.'

'He keeps photos of me in his wallet?' This time I took a gulp of water.

'You don't know? Lots of them. Let's face it, he just adores you.' Her eyes glistened with emotion. She prattled on about the nature of the photos, starting with one taken on our wedding day, while I sat by in a bit of a daze.

Before she finally got up to leave, she got in one more of those "Days of our Lives" comments. 'I said to Peter, on the way back, I said, if we can stay as much in love as they are, when we're married, I won't ask for more.'

I knew I was definitely in need of something stronger than water after she'd gone. My husband and I had, after all, recently embarked on discussions that would lead to the first phase of what turned out to be a long, and at times, acrimonious divorce. I also wondered what else I didn't know and was never likely to know about the man I'd lived with for so long.

* * *

Our marriage or life partners are probably the greatest teachers from whom we can learn. Or not. But until we become enlightened we tend to have preconceived ideas about our unions with them. These mostly revolve around "them" making "us" happy instead of "us" feeling happy within ourselves.

I had concerns about my husband's drinking and sporadic interest in sex before we got married but accepted his assertion that things would change for the better once we were married. I was of course devastated when this never happened. I believe, however, that we both initially assumed that because we had deep affection for one another and enjoyed each other's company that everything would work out. What we didn't factor into the equation was that many of the similarities we shared would only surface, in adverse ways, after our marriage.

For instance, as we weren't consciously aware that inner spirit beauty even existed, neither of us had any idea that we were both experiencing a feeling of disconnection from it. As a consequence we always felt something was missing from our relationship whereas in reality it was missing from ourselves. Initially we probably unconsciously believed, as most unenlightened couples do, that we'd discovered in each other "the one" who'd complete us. We felt let down, of course, when it proved not to be the case. As we are already one with our Maker, we are already complete and only once we understand this can we experience and appreciate love with others.

We also weren't consciously aware we'd both experienced separation anxiety shortly after our births. His mother suffered depression and had to go away to recover. Shirley remained in hospital to get over her ordeal. I believe these incidents contributed to us developing early abandonment complexes which resulted in us both fearing the leaving of our marriage more than staying in it.

Neither were we consciously aware that we both came from affection deprived backgrounds. This resulted in us desiring affection but in different ways. I was of the misguided belief that it came through sex. He on the other hand, while initially seeming to enjoy the demonstrative affection I showed him, was not that interested in sex. So he stopped giving me attention to avoid it and I stopped showing him I cared because I feared he'd interpret it as me wanting him to make love to me. Strangely enough he would totally amaze me on occasion by holding and kissing my hand while stroking my arm *in public* – but never in private where he no doubt worried his actions would be in jeopardy of having to end in what he appeared to fear most – intercourse.

He believed I was over-sexed and I believed he was asexual or at best had a low libido. Due to our lack of enlightenment, these beliefs were never discussed in a helpful way and may have contributed to him seeking comfort in increased alcohol consumption. We also mirrored each other perfectly. We didn't love ourselves so we were incapable of loving one another. We chose instead to blame each other and thereby, in effect, ourselves, for everything.

The irony is that if we'd both been enlightened beings when we first met, it's quite likely we wouldn't have even chosen one another for a one-night stand let alone marriage. There would have been no matching inadequacies and therefore nothing, quite frankly, for us to learn from one another. I would like to believe though that because we initially got on so well in so many ways that we would have become friends.

If I had found out, *shortly after I got married*, what I know now, I could have either run away as fast as possible or stayed, and through my knowledge, contributed to a more successful marriage. If I'd allowed myself to discover where my insecurities stemmed from and accepted that I'd brought them into my life to learn from them, I could've faced them, dealt with them and not held him responsible for them. To ensure that all this would've ended in a favourable marriage, however, would also have necessitated him joining me on the path to enlightenment. If, hypothetically, he had done so our combined realisations at the same time could have resulted in a more positive outcome.

It's therefore good to know that with knowledge at our collective disposal nobody needs to resort to divorce to overcome perceived insurmountable problems and insecurities. Provided both parties are committed to making their relationship work, all that's required is to simply become enlightened, by allowing ourselves to feel our connection with our Maker once more. Thereafter it will be as easy as it was when we were babies to also feel our inner spirit beauty again. And to reflect it outwards to show the love we really are, to everyone, including our partners. But most importantly to show it to ourselves.

# Chapter 14

# Torn to Shreds

'It hurts,' I cried.

'Don't be so utterly ridiculous, if you can't even accommodate a tampon, you'll *never* be able to accommodate a man.'

Shirley's words cut right through the pain and discomfort I was experiencing and opened another wound that took almost a lifetime to heal. *Is having sex going to be a very painful and awful experience?* I wondered about this with a combination of fear and trepidation. Shirley was "assisting" me to insert my first tampon and was enjoying the experience even less than I was.

It was a couple of weeks before my 12th birthday and it was turning out to be the worst day I'd so far experienced in my young life. I had woken up early with unusual cramps persistently gnawing away at the inside of my *tummy*. When I went to the bathroom I was horrified to discover I was actually bleeding to death. But when I rushed to inform Shirley of my highly anticipated demise, she seemed to think what was happening was completely normal. 'No, you're not about to die,' she laughed. 'Your periods have started that's all. Never mind, you'll get used to them in time. It's a curse all women have to put up with once a month for most of their lives. Have a bath and I'll bring you a tampon.'

Discovering that I was going to experience painful bleeding every month for a good portion of my life was seriously bad enough as revelations go – but the thought of enduring this regular unpleasantness while wearing an uncomfortable something called a "tampon" seemed like a double curse. Tampons, from what I had just gleaned from Shirley's comment, were not only designed to stem blood flow but also as a test to assess one's ability to accommodate men. It was altogether just too much for a not-quite twelve-year-old to suddenly take in.

'When do I have to accommodate the man?' I asked in wide-eyed innocence. Considering everything else that had happened so far that day I anticipated that this further ordeal was imminent. Judging by Shirley's response I might just as well have asked her permission to become a prostitute.

'What on earth are you talking about? Not before you're married of course,' she shouted. 'Don't even think about having sex until then. You don't want to end up getting pregnant and having a baby without a husband do you?' The first half of her response was a huge relief. The second half wasn't.

As you'll recall, my birth wasn't exactly a walk in the park for either Shirley or me and resulted in me being an only child. Her words constantly played in my head like a DVD on a loop. *'Ingrid tore me to shreds during her birth … who in their right mind would put themselves through that ghastly experience twice … if they knew what was in store for them … and could possibly avoid it?'*

Her sentiments regarding this issue were so deeply embedded in my psyche it's no wonder the awful vision I'd conjured up in my mind of being "torn to shreds" lingered with me throughout my childhood and continued into my adolescent and adult years.

So it stands to reason that of all the frightening things I was experiencing the day my periods started, the thought that I could now become pregnant, give birth and no doubt get "torn to shreds" in the process was undoubtedly the scariest.

* * *

Moving into my teens, however, as a veteran of monthly assaults by the odious red peril, and the accompanying use of the dreaded tampons, I somehow couldn't help my hormones from matching those of eager young admirers.

Despite my fear of getting pregnant and the anticipated horror that the ordeal of giving birth posed, I nonetheless found myself greatly enjoying all the attention I was receiving. Engaging in experimental kissing and touching was a new joy in my life and one which I totally confused with something that was largely missing from it, particularly following the death of my grandmother. Affection.

Accommodating my admirers in the full sexual act was, however, not on the agenda at all. Shirley had successfully put the fear of a very unmerciful God into me as regards that activity, also of the potential outcome of it. As a result I found myself holding on to my virginity, albeit by the skin of my teeth, for far longer than seemed to have been the case with most of my girlfriends. My chaste denial of taking affectionate exchanges, as I saw them, through to their natural conclusion soon resulted in me becoming the best little cock-tease this side of the equator.

When I did eventually throw caution to the wind, yet not without a deep underlying fear, I found "accommodating men" to be a bit of an anti-climax. Pun intended. To be truthful, although exciting and rewarding in varying degrees, I have never really enjoyed it quite as much as foreplay and the affection that goes with it.

The first time was like a movie everyone's been raving about for ages but which doesn't quite live up to its hype when you eventually experience it first-hand. However, no doubt the constant fear of getting pregnant and being torn to shreds giving birth always worriedly lurked in the back of my mind back then. It probably also set the tone for a lifetime of love making without the totally unbridled fireworks everyone else claims to experience as a matter of course or should I say intercourse. I suppose it's worth considering that maybe, sub-consciously, I've never ever completely surrendered and "let go" of the "being torn to shreds" association.

I have, however, always loved children, so coming to terms with the fact that the only way I was going to acquire any of my own was through childbirth did initially put me in a bit of a quandary.

*What is the alternative?* I pondered back then. Adopting didn't seem likely for a newly-married woman whose ability to conceive hadn't been fully tested through the normal channels of marital intercourse – because, as you already know, there wasn't any normal intercourse in my marriage.

I therefore began my quest, via affairs, as outlined in a previous chapter, for Mr Right while still married to Mr Wrong. This of course was in the hope of not only finding that perfect somebody who would, through his absolute wonderfulness, make me whole, but who would also father my children. If I had to get torn to shreds while giving birth, well … (deep breath) … I eventually came to the superficial conclusion … so be it. How does the saying go? Better to have tried and failed than never to have tried at all. Even if failing meant potentially becoming a shred of one's former self.

As you are also aware, Mr Right, when he did eventually arrive on the scene, simply turned out to be another Mr Wrong in disguise. This discovery was not before I decided to have an appointment with my gynae to arrange getting rid of my "IUD". My rationale was that I needed to be prepared to get pregnant with or without the consent of Mr Right. Maybe if I didn't tell him of my plans, and then announced I was pregnant, he would be so thrilled to hear he was going to become a father he'd immediately ditch his wife, with whom he didn't have children, and we'd live happily ever after. Then again, on reflection, maybe I needed to have my head examined rather than my vagina.

The gynaecological foray, however, put paid to all my fantasies about becoming a mother through giving birth to my own baby. I hadn't seen my gynae for a while so I was relieved that he even recognised me. Maybe not all vaginas look the same after all?

Following a thorough examination he determined that my IUD had been in position for such a protracted period of time that it had become part of me. *No wonder my period pains are getting worse by the month*, I thought. 'I can't imagine how you haven't got pregnant already,' the gynae announced. 'This device inside of you, which you have been euphemistically referring to as your IUD has totally overstayed its welcome – there's no way it could possibly be giving you any protection against conceiving whatsoever.'

So firmly embedded was it in fact that it could only be surgically removed with the aid of a DNC. It was during this procedure that it was unfortunately discovered that other things weren't looking that *kosher* down there either – especially for someone intent on becoming a mother.

My "cells" had apparently changed shape, a precursor, I was informed, to the big "C". As the female members of my family have a history of cancer in the nether regions of their anatomy, it was therefore determined that I required a hysterectomy as soon as yesterday. I was shocked beyond belief to receive this unwanted news and walked around talking to myself for days. 'What other catastrophe does the bloody universe have planned for me? It's just so unfair. Why me for God's sake?' *First a husband who's not interested in sex and by association in fathering children – and now this*, I thought.

'What the hell have I ever done to warrant this relentless bad *shit* in my life,' I screamed, and so on and so forth. I continued to shout various aspects of my displeasure loud and clear, using expletives that shouldn't be repeated.

Once I'd finished the tirade on all and sundry, including my Maker and was all cursed out, I made a decision. I decided my gynae must somehow have got it all wrong. His findings simply couldn't be right. So, based on that more plausible conclusion I set about getting two more opinions to confirm my belief.

'Are you absolutely sure this is necessary?' I said, or rather begged, for the third time. But the answer remained the same. They were all in agreement. It was imperative that I have a hysterectomy as soon as possible. And so it came about. My nursery was unceremoniously yanked out of me without further ado and replaced with a great big play pen of nothingness.

I felt totally abused and destroyed. Empty. There was no going back, however. Even the remotest chance of having a biological child of my own was no more. Finished. *Kaput.* I was now officially a childless person. Unlike a homeless person who always has an opportunity somehow, somewhere, to change their homeless status, my hysterectomy confirmed my childless status was permanent.

It was a bitter pill to swallow and blaming Shirley for creating an environment that "made me" averse to giving birth in the first place only provided temporary relief.

* * *

The strange thing is that the insight, which eventually brought about my comprehension of everything and that I was longing for, was initially rejected by me.

That insight was "We bring everything into our lives".

Up until my "Awakening" I unequivocally blamed everyone else for my unhappiness. I never stopped for even a second to contemplate that everything that was going wrong in my world was in any way of my doing. Or my fault. As far as I was concerned there was absolutely "no way" that I was to blame and to even suggest that this could be the case was an anathema I was not going to even entertain.

But … when I did stop and think about it in a rational, adult fashion, for the first time, well … it started to make sense. I was forced to come to the obvious conclusion that I and only I was the common denominator in every not so good situation I was experiencing or had ever experienced. As hard as that was to admit it also proved to be extremely cathartic and liberating as well – because as we all know, the truth sets us free.

I began to realise that it had started with my uneasy birth after I'd decided at the last minute that I didn't want to be born after all and which contributed to me being labelled as an asthmatic. It then progressed into my largely unhappy childhood when I excluded joyful people and experiences from my life – having decided the only joy I *needed* to experience was via my grandmother. It carried on into my insecure adulthood strewn with bad decisions and negative choices in friends and associates, but mainly in intimate relationships with men.

The reality, however, is that I'd drawn all these people into my life to teach me lessons I wanted to learn.

It also applied of course to my unhappy marriage and my decision to stay in it for fear of leaving it as well as the tragedy of denying myself children by drawing Shirley's paranoia into my life. And through even greater fear, bringing about the final nail in the coffin – the unconsciously orchestrated hysterectomy that made one hundred per cent certain there'd never be the remotest chance I'd ever be torn to shreds. And those are just a few examples.

* * *

If I'd learned the lessons I'd come to Planet Earth to be taught, sooner, I could have experienced a life filled with all the good stuff faster. But, as the saying goes, better late than never. When I finally came to terms with being the architect of my own demise it enabled me at long last to honestly address my negative situation in a positive way. Combined with other valuable insights that I had at last learned, my future started looking brighter virtually overnight, or as I prefer to refer to it, as "greatly enlightened" with expectation.

# Chapter 15

# Another Bite at a Vrot Cherry

'Do you still love me?' It was a pathetic question and a desperate plea for reassurance, all in one. 'I don't know.' My husband mumbled his irritated response without taking his eyes off the TV screen. 'But why do you have to bring it up now?' He was watching the men's semi-final at Wimbledon and was definitely not in the mood to delve into my insecurities. Then again I can't think of a time when he ever was. And on reflection, many years later, I wondered why I had ever thought he would be. After all, it never occurred to me to delve into his insecurities because quite simply he never believed he had any.

Following his response to my question anyone in their right mind would no doubt have walked, nay run at great speed, straight out of the marriage there and then. But, as I was far from being in my right mind, following the events or non-events of our honeymoon and subsequent life together, I simply allowed his response to confirm all the inadequacies and short-comings I had started feeling about myself. If he didn't know whether he still loved me so soon after getting married, maybe he never loved me at all? Or maybe nobody could love me or would ever love me? Those were just some of the dark thoughts I entertained. It's amazing what unhinged minds can dish up to themselves when their lack of awareness of being one with the love of their maker allows them to buy into all manner of hurtful utterances and actions of others.

What I didn't know then of course was that neither I nor my husband could have expected to be loved by the other because quite simply we didn't love ourselves at that time. We didn't love ourselves because we'd lost all feeling of connection with our inner spirit beauty – to the extent that we had no memory of it ever existing.

It was a few months into our marriage and we'd just returned from a holiday in Zimbabwe – a generous birthday present to my husband from his parents. It wasn't a gift to me of course, but by virtue of my new status as his wife I too, by association, became a recipient of it. If you think that's a strange thing to say you need to appreciate that my feeling of disconnection from my inner spirit beauty, and resultant loss of love for myself, managed to adversely affect my relationships with just about everyone else. Including his family with whom I never experienced a particularly close connection.

I had secretly hoped the holiday might offer us an opportunity for a second honeymoon. Another bite at the cherry if you like. As it turned out however the cherry had already gone bad or as is better described in the very expressive language of Afrikaans, the cherry was now *vrot.* So the time away simply proved to be a fruitless attempt to correct the mistakes of the original fiasco and to live happily ever after. In fact the close proximity we found ourselves in 24/7 during the period only seemed to highlight the ever-widening chasm between us.

The beauty of Victoria Falls, the magnificent wild life at Wankie and the splendour of Kariba were all dulled for me by the constant pain of the unfulfilled life I was now living and that in no way improved with a change of scene.

# Chapter 16

# Divorced from the Family

In addition to the alienation of affection from my husband that I allowed myself to endure, there was also the "not quite welcome" feeling I experienced from his family – despite there being an ever-present veneer of cordiality. They were an unusually close bunch who I realised, but unfortunately not until after my marriage, didn't willingly encourage "outsiders" into the bosom of their tightly knit clan.

One of my husband's cousins did, however, share with me that an exception might have been made if any members of the British Royal Family had shown an interest in marrying my husband or his sisters. But no exceptions were ever going to be made in the case of local yocals like myself and my brother-in-law, who married the younger of my husband's sisters. We were mainly tolerated, I felt, in varying degrees but were never totally welcomed as full members of the family.

The closest I came to a relationship with any of them was with my husband's eldest sister who I took an instant liking to the first time we met. Despite a big age difference, we not only shared a similar sense of humour but also an appreciation for good looking male movie stars and cricketers – vital ingredients that translated into amusing observations and discussions on a variety of topics, related and otherwise. Even with her though, I still experienced a certain reserve and of course her total disappearance from my life following the divorce.

The uncomfortable distance that existed between me and his family first became obvious when I presented my mother-in-law with our wedding photos and asked her if she'd like to place an order for any of them. She thanked me and immediately made her selections. She chose two of my husband making his wedding speech, from different angles, and a group photo featuring her, my father-in-law, my two sisters-in-law and my husband. I was noticeably absent from her choices. The same applied to photos of her daughter's wedding. A group photo excluding the groom took pride of place on her mantelpiece along with the aforementioned photos of my wedding.

This strange behaviour didn't stop there unfortunately. It was particularly in evidence when my in-laws who were elderly parents to my husband took ill and passed away in quick succession. Just as Shirley and Bill had me late in life so too did my husband's parents have him late – but even later still – in fact quite some time after the births of his two sisters.

My father-in-law was the first to go and my husband informed me that the funeral would be held down at the coast close to their once family home.

'It won't take place until the end of the week, of course, but I'll have to go down there soonest to help with the arrangements.'

'Of course,' I said, 'When do we go, I'll have to arrange leave?'

'Oh no,' he looked at me askance, 'there's no need for *you* to come. I just want to be with my mother and my sisters. We need to be together at a time like this.'

I was amazed by my husband's lack of interest in sharing his grief with me. 'But surely you want me to go with you to … to support you?'

'Why do you always have to think of yourself,' he snapped in anger. 'It's *my* father who's died, not *yours*. Just respect what other people want for a change.'

Instead of walking away from it, which is what I should have done, I phoned his aunt, his mother's sister, and asked her what I was supposed to do in a situation that seemed quite odd to me. She didn't sound surprised at what had transpired, muttering something about them being unusually close, but suggested that the right thing to do would be for me to attend the funeral, regardless.

On the strength of that advice I phoned Bill and Shirley, advised them of the death in the family and told them I would be flying down to Durban at the end of the week. On arrival the three of us travelled by car from the airport to the funeral. We sat at the back of the church with other "non-family" members and took our place in the queue to offer our condolences to the "family". Feeling like interlopers we didn't linger for refreshments afterwards but drove straight back to Durban. I flew home on my own the following day.

My presence at the funeral was never discussed, it was, however, one of the strangest experiences of my life. But, on reflection, one entirely in keeping with the aloofness mostly shown to me by the family I'd married into, and of course, in particular, by my husband.

* * *

Not too long after his father's death, his mother passed away. The funeral took place in Gauteng where she had been living since the death of my father-in-law. This time I did crack an invite. However, as one of the cousins had come up from the coast for the funeral, and was staying with us, I suspected that it would have been awkward to exclude me. Or maybe I was included because his mother had bonded with me "ever so slightly" since my father-in-law's passing.

Despite our bonding she gave me my customary bar of soap for Christmas. It was a gift I'd received from her every year since the beginning of our relationship. I couldn't help thinking, with amusement, that it put a distinct question mark over my personal hygiene. My husband by contrast always received an unwavering gift of R1000, without inflation ever being factored in over time. Nothing was obviously perceived to be suspect about his hygiene I noted with equal amusement.

I was forced to come to the conclusion that my far from penny-less yet ultra-frugal mother-in-law viewed the giving of presents as an *unnecessary* evil and considered the least time spent on the chore of choosing them the better. This was confirmed and best illustrated by a very "unusual" Christmas present that she gifted Shirley with one year.

We were having Christmas day celebrations at the home of my mother-in-law's brother and were gathered en masse in the garden under a large shady tree as a big pile of presents were doled out one by one to the intended recipients.

What at first appeared to be a shoe box wrapped in festive paper was handed to Shirley, who on reading the card nodded her thanks accompanied by a smile in the direction of my mother-in-law as she set about unwrapping it. As the last remnants of the paper fell away from the box housing the gift it revealed itself, however, not to be a shoe box at all but an extra-large economy box of Twin Saver tissues. 'Oh,' said a disbelieving and shell-shocked Shirley who prided herself on only ever choosing and giving quality presents, 'Oh … Oh … how … how, lovely.'

Aside from her thrifty gift choices I couldn't help but feel sorry for my mother-in-law when she lost her husband. I took her to the theatre, which she loved, on a couple of occasions to jolly up her life, had her around for meals and invented a fictitious boyfriend for her who I named "Rupert". I would often tease her in this regard. 'What are you and Rupert up to this weekend, anything exciting?'

'Oh Ingrid, stop it, stop it.' She'd always protest but laugh with genuine pleasure at the notion of the mythical Rupert.

All this being said it was still surprising that the unfortunate circumstances of her death didn't totally mitigate against me being allowed to attend her funeral – regardless of the cousin from the coast who was staying at our home in order to attend it.

* * *

When my mother-in-law first took ill, following a bad dose of flu that turned to pneumonia and resulted in her being rushed to hospital, I was subjected to the same alienation I'd experienced following my father-in-law's death.

'Mum's very ill – she's just been admitted to hospital and I'm on my way there now. I don't know what time I'll be back.'

My husband was in a state of total shock. 'Oh my God, I'm so sorry … would you like me to … to go with you?' In view of the past experience relating to me being barred from anything to do with his father's departure from this world, I worded my question in trepidation.

'Absolutely not, my sisters and I just want to be with her on our own.' This time I was prepared and not in the least bit phased to hear of my exclusion. I offered no resistance at all. In fact, in line with the abnormal life my husband and I were now living, his response seemed completely normal.

He and his sisters spent days and nights at his mother's bedside, over a period of about a week, taking turns to go home now and then to get some sleep.

As time went by and her condition worsened, according to the odd account of it I managed to extract from my husband, I began to wonder if she'd ever thought it strange that I had never visited her. How though would she even know that I'd been discouraged from doing so?

I shared my thoughts about this with my good friend Trevor over lunch on the Saturday following her hospital admission. Trevor as it turned out had a strong point of view regarding the matter. 'You've got to go and see her as soon as possible,' he emphatically announced. 'You'll never forgive yourself if you don't and she dies.'

I've never been quite sure whether it was the first bottle of wine we shared, or the second that changed the complexion of the day. Yet shortly after imbibing my last glass I found myself racing at great speed to the hospital in my little Italian sports car – a newly acquired perk associated with my advertising job.

It must have been the adrenalin rush of the drive in my uncustomary state of inebriation behind the wheel, during which I showed total disregard for speed limits while relishing the responsive handling of my new car, because I felt remarkably sober on arrival. I was, however, in no way prepared for the exhausted and ghostly appearances of my husband and his sisters. My mother-in-law looked quite well by comparison even though she was now in ICU.

If they were shocked to see *me* they must have all been too tired to show it.

'Gosh,' I said, 'you all look completely wacked. Why don't you just let me sit with her for a bit while you go and have a cup of tea and maybe something to eat … in the restaurant?' To my surprise they didn't resist my suggestion and filed out of her cubicle like a troop of ultra-exhausted zombies.

My mother-in-law who was plugged into an ECG machine lay motionless yet serene and peaceful on her hospital bed as I took one of her hands in mine. I hoped that she may in some way be able to feel my presence. 'I'm sad,' I said, 'that it's taken me this long to come and visit you … especially as we seem to have grown closer over the past year. I … I'd just like you to know that although our relationship hasn't always been easy, for either of us … I'm terribly sorry that you're so ill … it's my dearest wish that you somehow find the strength to get through this … and make a full recovery ...'

With that the ECG machine that had been happily bleeping along at an even pace simply flat lined.

I was totally horrified as I jumped to my feet and started screaming for the nursing staff. They arrived in record time and quickly ushered me out of her cubicle as they attempted, in vain as it turned out, to perform a resuscitation.

*Oh my God, why did I come here? Did I inadvertently cause her death?* These were some of my frantic thoughts as I asked one of the nurses to inform my husband and his sisters to return to her ward as soon as possible. I by contrast swiftly made my way back to my car. I knew in my heart that I would be the very last person they would wish to share their grief with.

* * *

The thoughts that occupied my mind for years following her death were these: Did she decide to go because she couldn't stand the thought of being left alone with me? Or had she perhaps been waiting for me to visit her so she could happily depart this lifetime in the knowledge that all was well between us?

Based on my spiritual awakening, and the knowledge gained as a result of it I eventually chose, with conviction I may add, to believe the latter.

Even though I hadn't recaptured my own inner spirit beauty, through a feeling of re-connection with my Maker at the time of her death I have come to the conclusion that my elderly mother-in-law had recaptured hers.

# Chapter 17

# What We Resist Persists

'Your mother has had another bad fall. We've moved her to frail care but we're waiting for an ambulance to take her and her caregiver to the hospital. She'll need to have x-rays of course … we suspect fractures.'

My mother broke bones at such a rate I secretly wondered why the retirement village didn't just make a standard recording regarding these and play it to me every few months. Or maybe they had and the cordial finale … "Let us know the outcome … whether she'll be staying in hospital, returning to frail care or to her house. Thanks Ingrid, take care." … was simply part of the recording.

How many more fractures could her frail body handle? That was the first thing that always crossed my mind. The second was selfishly the same one that always reared its ugly head after hearing of my mother's latest broken bone or bones. 'Oh my God what more can I do to positively ensure this never happens to me?'

Shirley had been falling and breaking bones for as long as I could remember. The first, as I recall, was a broken wrist when she was in her late 30s. Then there was the broken arm in her early 40s and a premature hip replacement in her 50s … and so on and so forth right up to her last break.

* * *

'Your mother's bones are like honeycombed crunchy bars.' These were the startling words delivered by the specialist surgeon who was attending her following her first fall in Gauteng after relocating from the coast. 'It's as a result of a combination of factors, of course, starting with the intravenous cancer treatment she received following her hysterectomy – it's all here in her records.' He thumped the large brown envelope that had been couriered up from the coast for emphasis.

We were seated in his office at his expensive mahogany desk with the parcel containing Shirley's medical history lying between us. I felt nauseas. 'Oh how wonderfully put.' The words spontaneously slipped out of my mouth. Hoping that my shocked response hadn't sounded too sarcastic I tried to correct my initial statement but in so doing probably made things worse. 'You've got a natural gift for words … I've never heard her bones described like that before.'

He, however, didn't seem to notice and simply droned on in his uncharismatic way. 'Yes, well, that treatment she had combined with the fact that she has been a heavy smoker most of her life, doesn't eat much, doesn't exercise at all and drinks far too much tea, doesn't help either.' He leaned forward confidentially. 'You need to take care of yourself you know. Small, fair-haired, blue eyed women who've never had children are excellent candidates for osteopenia followed by osteoporosis.'

'Gosh aren't I the lucky one? Do I score any brownie points for having given up smoking and disliking tea?' I thumped the brown envelope for emphasis as he had done and gave him a quizzical look.

He sort of responded with a bit of a laugh and a snort combo but I sensed he didn't have a great sense of humour. 'I'm afraid to say, no … not really. There's also the "Genes Factor" to contend with.' He massaged his clean-shaven chin. 'Your mother mentioned that your maternal grandmother wasn't gifted with great bones either.' I nodded and he shrugged his shoulders. 'My advice to you is, eat as many calcium rich foods as possible and exercise as often as you can.'

'What about hormone replacement?' I enquired in the hope that some magical potion could prevent me from developing these unwanted diseases.

'Too soon for that, we'll talk about it again in a few years.' With that he stood up, indicating our meeting was over.

* * *

The meeting was over but my concern over the future health of my bones had only just begun. From that moment on I became obsessed with their preservation. I read everything I could on the subject, changed my diet to include calcium-enriched vegetables and salads, and started exercising for the first time in my adult life. I hadn't realised until the specialist's "pep talk" just how much of a lounge lizard I really was. Just like Shirley.

But, unlike Shirley, I was not going to become a sufferer of broken bones. Oh no, not me, I was now on a crusade to prove that Shirley and I couldn't be less alike in that department. Oops. Famous last words.

I accepted an email generated invitation to join a gym close to where I lived with as much enthusiasm as a turkey accepting an invitation to Christmas dinner. I never failed to remind myself, however, on every day of my unhappy attendance that I was there to ensure I would never suffer from broken bones.

Then I went on a Sunday hike in the Magaliesberg and broke my first bone. We were crossing a trickle of water that was supposed to represent a stream when, demonstrating my newly-found gym-induced athleticism, I slipped on a wet rock as I attempted to jump over it. My husband, with good intentions, leapt to my rescue by grabbing my arm and pulling it in an unnatural upward movement to save me from getting my ankles wet.

In so doing, and without either of us knowing at the time, the top of my scapula cracked under the unusual pressure. The pain was excruciating but everyone present was of the opinion I'd simply torn a muscle – including the physiotherapist who attended to me on the Monday morning. She was situated in rooms close to the Rosebank Clinic so after two tearful physio appointments I took myself to the clinic for an x-ray that confirmed my hairline fracture and the potential fragility of my bones. I couldn't believe it. I'd started *gym* for God's sake and ate lots of *salad,* don't you know? How could this happen to me?

Thereafter, and because nobody would accept me for hormone replacement therapy at that time, I consulted a professor who came highly recommended as an expert in the field of genetically wonky bones. He agreed to prescribe a preventative medication that was currently all the rage in Europe. Sadly, this medication proved to be the bane of my life in the long term, as it was eventually discovered that it didn't in fact treat bones from the inside – instead it hardened them with a false coating on the outside. In so doing it simply prevented x-rays and even bone density scans from providing true readings.

As a result I lived in a fool's paradise for sometime until I was finally prescribed a bisphosphonate medication. That is when my real bone problems began and my long-held belief that medications were going to be the solution to my bone problems simply crumbled. All the medication did in effect was to prevent my bones from performing their own regeneration. This, coupled with the discredited preventative treatment which was still recording hardened bones on the exterior resulted in the cultivation of ultra-brittle bones on the interior. The kind that cracked and fractured easily. The age old saying, what you resist persists could have been written just for me.

* * *

'So maybe it wasn't such a good idea to try a new route in this bad weather but …'

'Oh how right you are,' I interrupted in sarcastic irritation.

'Okay, but I had no idea the rain was going to be this relentless,' he said, sounding guilty as charged. 'Anyway we're here now. Just stay put and I'll go and get the key from reception.'

Back then my husband and I had just arrived for our annual visit to an out-of-the-way resort on the Transkei Wild Coast, after a tortuous car journey in the rain through what had seemed like endless mud and slush.

'Don't worry I'm in no hurry to go anywhere until you can tell me exactly which bungalow we're staying in and the quickest route to get to it.' All I wanted was a nice hot shower and a change of clothes.

He was over the moon when he returned with the key. 'We've got the bungalow I wanted … the one right on the beach … and the rain's eased up quite a bit, so let's make a dash for it – I'll come back for the rest of our things later.'

We started to make our way down to the beach clutching our bare essentials. At the same time, a few murky sunbeams were bravely starting to cut their way through the clouds in a successful attempt to keep the rain down to a light drizzle.

My spirits began to lift in appreciation of the good work of the sunbeams, when all too suddenly I was rudely reminded that I had nothing whatsoever to be happy about. Taking my eyes off the moss laden stepping-stones in favour of admiring the sunbeams, albeit for a brief moment, was all it took to bring about my downfall.

I not only lost my footing but my ability to prevent myself from falling too. My outstretched arm and hand seemed to take on a life of their own. The rest of me was dragged along behind them as they skidded along the ground and crunched to a stop under my weight.

As I scrambled to my feet with the aid of my left hand and arm, I couldn't help noticing that my right hand now seemed to be greeting me in an unnatural upward facing position. A sort of static royal wave if you like. Unfamiliar as I was with broken wrists at the time, I foolishly tried to straighten it and that's when the excruciating and relentless pain began.

I just couldn't believe that despite all the precautions I'd taken I had just managed, single-handedly, to notch up a second fracture.

So it was back into the car and off in the direction of the closest towns we travelled in search of a medical facility. When we arrived at the nearest hospital fate took a hand – my hand. 'Hey boy, what're *you* doing here?' It was the exuberant cry of delight from an old friend of my husband who, as it turned out, just happened to be the resident gynaecologist.

'I don't believe it, *howzit* man,' replied my equally happy husband as he eyed his friend's white coat. 'Are you working here?'

'I absolutely am, been the resident gynae for a couple of years now – it's the life my man, I can tell you.'

Before he could explain why it was the life I interjected with a pain-induced moan in order to remind my husband why indeed we were at the hospital in the first place. I was hastily introduced and the reason for my plight explained – fortunately his friend didn't want to shake hands.

'Well you've come to the right place,' he exclaimed with enthusiasm. 'I'll sort out that wrist of yours in a tick.'

'No disrespect,' I managed to say, in between the jabs of exquisite pain throbbing through my wrist and arm, 'but I'd prefer to see an orthopod.'

'Sorry to tell you but we just don't have one here, but don't worry, I've set many bones, don't think yours is the first. I can see you're in pain so let's get you admitted and sorted with a painkiller then we can arrange your surgery.'

I was in far too much pain to argue and as a result allowed myself to buy into what he was proposing – besides, the promise of a painkiller was the final clincher. After an ultra-speedy admission, he administered the promised relief intravenously and I sailed out of my pain-wracked body into pain free heaven from where I reluctantly awoke many hours later.

I felt super woozy and generally out of sorts as one would expect following surgery. But the most disappointing aspect of all was that my wrist still ached and was now incarcerated in an old-fashioned Plaster of Paris cast that weighed a ton and covered most of my hand and much of my forearm.

My husband also appeared out of sorts when he arrived a short while later. It transpired that he and "my surgeon" had decided to hit the town, so to speak, in order to celebrate their reunion brought about courtesy of my broken wrist. I'm sure there wasn't much more to hit in the area other than the local shebeen but judging by my husband's still mildly hungover state it must have been well stocked with beer.

'How are you, ready to leave?' He smiled at me enthusiastically, no doubt happy at the thought of resuming his holiday. 'Yes, I'm ready to leave … for Joburg, so I can get my wrist, that's still sore by the way, checked out by a proper bone specialist.'

His mood changed in a flash. 'You're crazy, you know? Naturally it's still sore, it's just been operated on. If you think I'm driving all the way back to Joburg today you're out of your mind.'

'Okay,' I said with resignation as I tried to lift my overweight cast in order to sit up straighter against my pillows. 'We can go back to the resort today … but I want to go back to Joburg tomorrow … at the latest.'

He punched his right fist into the palm of his left hand in anger and glared at me. 'You have got to be the most selfish person in the world. You know how much I've been looking forward to this holiday. And now you're intent on spoiling it for me from beginning to end.'

'Well I'm so sorry that I fell and broke my wrist but I'm even more sorry that I allowed your "friend" to operate on it. You should have looked out for me and made sure we found an orthopaedic surgeon … somewhere, even … even if we had to drive to another town.'

'You needed urgent attention,' he shouted. 'Now pull yourself together and let's get out of here, I can think of better places to spend the day.' And that was that. We returned to our Wild Coast Resort and stayed there for the duration of our booking. Two weeks.

"Pull yourself together" by the way was one of my husband's favourite comments and was always extended to me when I shared any concerns with him about anything and everything. It was therefore no surprise that it was conveyed to me in this instance. He also made it known that he felt it was time I stopped thinking about myself and put him first "for a change" by mastering the art of getting by for a couple of weeks with a sore hand. 'Besides,' he'd stated, 'everyone else has now arrived and they're all looking forward to seeing you.'

* * *

It was something I did a lot of in those days. I put on a good show of enjoying myself for all our friends who visited the same resort as us every year at the same time, but if truth be known, I really had a desperately unhappy time of it. As the "holiday" progressed in the uncomfortable heat of a Transkei Wild Coast summer, not designed for those clothed in heavy old-fashioned Plaster of Paris casts, it became more and more evident that *my* cast had been incorrectly placed.

I munched my way through every painkiller in sight but my wrist remained painful and could now move at will in all directions within the cast without any proper re-alignment support whatsoever. Although my complaints in this regard continued, they fell on deaf ears. On returning home it was no surprise to discover that my wrist was in a bad way. It had to be re-broken and reset by a "proper" bone specialist. 'This was a bad break to start with, sorry, I had to repeat the process.' The orthopod shook his head with regret. 'I don't know what possessed a gynaecologist to take on the job.'

I nodded in agreement but resisted the temptation to let on that the gynae's major incentive had been to spend the evening with my husband enjoying a mammoth "when we" session over copious beers.

* * *

All my subsequent fractures happened just prior to my divorce, and following it, during the setting up of the film company my first post advertising business. It was at that time that I added intense running and jogging to my "prevent-breaking-bones-at-all-costs" regime. As it turned out all this managed to achieve was to conclusively reinforce that what one resists definitely persists.

It started with a broken left wrist, to match the right wrist break sustained on the Transkei Wild Coast and occurred while jogging close to home. Other wrist fractures occurred at regular intervals

– one while running in a race and another while jogging with my dog at Zoo Lake. Up to that point I'd notched up four wrist fractures in total – two left, two right. There was nothing unbalanced about me. More however were still to come.

Being unenlightened back then, I didn't realise at the time or the time after that, that my string of bone fractures had little or nothing to do with bad genes inherited from Shirley. They had so much more to do with the negative situations I was constantly drawing into my life at regular intervals. Mostly in the area of unfavourable relationships.

As I may have mentioned before, every happy or unhappy incident in life is a mirror image of what we are experiencing within ourselves at any given moment via the vibrations that we emit. Low vibrations attract the not so good happenings while high vibrations are responsible for the good ones. And unfortunately for me it was low vibrations that were overtaking me at that time.

Until I woke up to that there was just nothing stopping broken bones from being regularly drawn into my world. A constant reminder that my life in general wasn't in great shape courtesy of all the negativity that I was failing to transform into positivity. Added to that, by working as hard as I was at "trying" to prevent my bones from fracturing, I was actually working against the natural flow of the Universe to ensure that they would continue to be an ever present feature of my life. This state of mind that I was experiencing also prevented the Universe, that can only identify with positivity, from being able to recognise and provide me with what I really "wanted". A fracture free life.

Every single broken bone I experienced was like a separate wake-up call. The first wrist fracture at the Wild Coast was alerting me to my unhappy marriage and urging me to do something about it – a wake-up call that I did eventually heed but should have acted on a lot sooner. All subsequent fractures were further wake-up calls designed to get my attention regarding enjoying life as opposed to working myself into the ground. And, as a result, falling into it too.

After finally acknowledging the "all-work-and-no-play" lifestyle I was busy carving out for myself, to the exclusion of life itself, I eventually woke up sufficiently to admit that I was on a downward spiral. I was therefore forced to make a decision, based on these insights, to turn my life around by adopting a new positive approach to it.

I stopped taking the medications and chose instead to nourish my body with appropriate supplements, healthy food, love, proper sleep, less work and a gentler but more effective exercise routine.

In more recent times my "Awakening" has also played an integral part by placing me and my body in harmony with the Universe and thereby with myself. My bones as result of this have not only stabilised but have become fracture free.

# Chapter 18

# Inner Beauty Can't be Achieved by Cosmetic Surgery

I left the advertising industry to start a film company that crashed and burned before it even got off the ground, but only after a lot of hard work, money and commitment had gone into it. I was naturally devastated at the time and played the usual blame game with everyone else involved in the venture. I told myself that its demise couldn't possibly have had anything to do with *me* as *I* had done everything possible to ensure its success. Yet just like all the things I've brought into my life I was, following my awakening, forced to accept my contribution to its failure.

When the initial concept on which we'd based the launch of the company proved to be flawed, I was reluctant to admit the undertaking was doomed. Instead of acknowledging this and allowing it to fold without incurring any further financial burden, I immediately started working on an alternative strategy to "try" and force it to work.

As "trying" falls into the same category as "needing", I was once more, in my unenlightened state, working against the Universe and preventing what I "wanted" for the company from materialising. When my new strategy also failed to save the day, I was, although I didn't know it at the time, undoubtedly the biggest contributor to the company's downfall costing us more than was necessary.

What was even more alarming at the time was the poor state of my personal finances. I, like my business partner, had sunk more than a little cash into the now defunct film company. Apart from that and my day to day living expenses, I now also found myself heading for the divorce court with demanding lawyer's bills following close on my heels. The cold reality of a bleak money-strapped future loomed large.

I was, therefore, forced to come to terms with the fact that I had to start earning again as quickly as possible. I wasn't quite sure at that juncture just exactly how I was going to do that but I felt certain, nevertheless, after the tough knock the failure of the film company had delivered, that something good had to be on the horizon.

The inspiration for my next business venture, this time one that proved to be a far more financially rewarding one, came about over dinner with a doctor friend. He was living in the UK but was holidaying back in South Africa at the time. 'Have you heard about medical tourism? It's fast becoming the new big thing in Europe.' He casually made this remark as he scanned the menu for his main course of choice.

'Oh really … and … and what exactly is medical tourism all about?' I found myself replying distractedly while trying to decide between the salmon and … I eventually opted for the grilled calamari.

'It's all come about due to the long wait everyone in the UK is experiencing when trying to get procedures performed on the National Health. People have discovered that they can go to places like Spain or even to countries in Eastern Europe and have their hip replacement or whatever done almost immediately.' He clicked his fingers to demonstrate the speed at which procedures could be performed outside of the UK. He laughed. 'I've been thinking about changing my name to Luigi and opening a practice in Spain.'

'Sorry to tell you but if you're dead set on that name you'll have to open a practice in Italy. Luigi as far as I know is not a Spanish name.' 'Oh okay, I'll have to work on the name.'

We were both laughing as we placed our respective orders but I suddenly found myself far hungrier for more information regarding medical tourism than I was for calamari. 'But surely it's an expensive alternative for patients. They get their procedures performed totally free on National Health don't they?'

'Actually, operations are surprisingly affordable in those countries but obviously not as cheap as on the National Health. It's hard to beat almost no charge at all. I guess it boils down to this. If you've got a bit of spare cash and are suffering from extreme discomfort while waiting goodness knows how long to have your procedure, you might be inclined to go elsewhere for your surgery.'

As he topped up our wine glasses, he also delivered the final determining factor that led to my decision. 'What's more, if they plan it right, they also get to escape the grim UK weather and experience a nice little holiday in the sunshine at the same time.'

So that dear friends, was the beginning of my next business venture – this time in the medical tourism business. I had quickly worked out however that arranging hip and knee replacements were not going to be my *main* focus. After some equally rapid yet seriously in-depth research I discovered that cosmetic surgery was a far more appealing option on which to concentrate my attention. It was fast attracting millions of eager followers throughout the world, and as it turned out was an instant drawcard to sunny South Africa.

The interest shown not only came from the UK and the US but from many other parts of the world too. It wasn't exclusively due to the acknowledged expertise of South African surgeons but was also as a result of our very affordable cosmetic surgery procedures provided courtesy of an exceptionally attractive exchange rate. Not to mention the abundance of beautiful and affordable holiday destinations on offer in sunny South Africa pre and post-surgery that could also be enjoyed courtesy of the same waning currency.

It's strange though that someone like myself, who always felt so uncomfortable in my own skin, should embark on a business dedicated to making others feel comfortable in theirs. Well, anyway, that is what I thought at the time. Now of course, following my awakening, I realise only too well that my cosmetic surgery-orientated business proved to be a very important feature of this lifetime of mine. It came about in fact in order to teach me one of my most valuable lessons.

After all, without being submerged in the business as I came to be for a good number of years, it would have been most unlikely that I would have otherwise come into contact with so many souls as insecure as myself.

I could of course provide you with many case studies relating to countless individual reasons that drove my clients, male and female, to desire cosmetic surgery. That, however, would be unfair on all who entrusted their vulnerable selves to me in confidence. They were confidences I totally respected then, and now, and which were extended to me in the hope that I, probably the most vulnerable of all at the time, would introduce them to the right medical practitioners for their needs. To those surgeons who would miraculously transform them into images of what they thought they should look like in order to be seen and loved as beautiful beings.

Rather than discussing any of my clients with you, even under pseudonyms, I am instead going to relate a little story that will give you some idea of a very general psychology people who desire cosmetic surgery present with. In reality however the real desire to change ourselves externally simply stems from experiencing a feeling of disconnection from our Maker and our inner spirit beauty, and as a result, from a misguided belief that beauty is external.

The story concerns a woman who had unfortunately been in an unhappy marriage for most of her life. She'd contemplated divorce many times of course yet as her husband was particularly well heeled, and she was more concerned with financial security over personal happiness, she continued to stay with him year after year. Their relationship naturally went from bad to worse, making the overall quality of her life less than desirable. Eventually, however, she was rewarded for her long and patient wait. His health took a dive, he became ill and eventually died of his condition, leaving her very comfortably off. She was for the first time in a very long while totally ecstatic with happiness and congratulated herself for hanging in with him for so many miserable years.

This was until she looked in the mirror long and hard and realised that the years of unhappiness she'd experienced had unfortunately taken their toll on what had once been considered her "good looks".

So she made a decision there and then to consult a plastic surgeon without delay to discuss a complete re-make of herself from head to toe. As she could afford everything that she wanted to have done, it wasn't long before she found a surgeon who agreed to accommodate all her "make-over" desires. It was not going to be a walk in the park though, the surgeon advised her, and would necessitate quite a few surgeries and a fair amount of discomfort too. She, however, rationalised that in order to truly enjoy her new-found wealth she would need to look younger and more appealing once more in order to attract desirable companions with whom to enjoy life to the full.

Without further ado she arranged to be booked into the clinic for her series of procedures to commence. Naturally, as there was so much to accomplish, she was there for quite a while before the full make-over was finally complete. Eventually the great day arrived when, looking a good 10-15 years younger, she emerged from the clinic.

She had a few reservations here and there but was generally happy with the results of all her surgeries and could hardly wait to go shopping for a new wardrobe to complement the new her. So instead of going home to rest, as she had been advised to do by her surgeon, she decided to start her shopping spree immediately. But fate took a nasty turn. As she walked off the premises of the clinic and started to cross the road in order to reach the shopping mall on the other side, a great big truck came round the corner. It was travelling far faster than it should have been in a built-up area and literally took her out.

Shocked and panic-stricken, she was met by her Maker at her after-life destination. 'For God's sake,' she angrily snapped, 'what on earth is going on? Don't you know that having spent countless years enduring a loveless marriage with that awful man, I've just paid a fortune getting a total cosmetic makeover so I can enjoy life at long last. What, pray tell, is your excuse for allowing me to be run over by a great big truck just as I was about to embark on the shopping adventure of my life?'

God looked at her quizzically at first and then responded. 'I'm terribly sorry, but to tell you the truth I just didn't recognise you.'

Jokes aside, if the aforementioned story featured a real person who had lived such a spiritually devoid life for so long, she may have been better served to make her re-unification with her Maker and inner spirit beauty her priority. And thereby have put herself in a position to reflect her true beauty from the inside out – even to the extent that she may have decided to give all the surgery she was planning a miss.

The answer is "no" in case you were wondering if my spiritual awareness has transformed me into an ex-advocator of plastic surgery. There will always be a place for it as it has so much to offer so many people.

The only change in my thinking on the subject is the one I became aware of following my awakening and subsequent enlightenment. I now also recommend this: if possible try not to change your appearance in any way by means of surgery, stringent dieting or any other manipulation of your appearance until such time as you have rekindled your relationship with your Maker. When you've re-established that special association you will also be able to feel your connection with the inner spirit beauty with which you were born – and that will give you the opportunity to reflect it outwards again for all to appreciate and reflect back to you.

It will also result in you being able to demonstrate restored feelings of love, security, joy, fulfilment, peace and satisfaction.

It therefore follows that this would also be the best time to avail yourself of any physical adjustment you may still desire – as your general feeling of well-being will also enable you to acknowledge whatever procedure you may choose to have performed as merely an enhancement of the already beautiful you. You'll also be in a position to fully enjoy it without fear of possible future disappointment with the outcome.

To attempt any "outward" beautification prior to being in the right space however could well lead to unhappiness with it in the long term. This is because, regardless of the end result of your surgery, if you're still feeling a disassociation from your Maker and inner spirit beauty, there's a good chance you may eventually come to feel "let-down" by it. You may even start to consider, due to your feelings of incompleteness, that whatever you had performed "didn't work". And, as a result, that you should begin looking for further sources of outer enhancement to make yourself look "better". After all, we cannot successfully display beauty on the outside without first "feeling" it on the inside. The place where true beauty comes from.

# Part 5

# Understanding Life With Love

# Chapter 19

# Walking in Shirley's Shoes

'Your mother has had another bad fall and unfortunately her caregiver isn't on duty. How soon can you get here? She's in a bad way both mentally and physically, so I thought it best if you take her to the hospital for the x-rays she needs rather than putting her in an ambulance on her own …? As usual we suspect fractures.'

The words of the matron at the retirement village, delivered via a cell call, were totally off script. Where was my mother's caregiver? She was supposed to be on duty. It was Saturday and she was only supposed to be off duty on the Sunday of that weekend. That was the day I had planned to visit my parents, take them their weekly groceries and make them lunch.

A call to my father revealed the answer. The caregiver had been invited to a wedding and had asked if she could swop her day off from Sunday to Saturday. My mother had graciously agreed but had neglected to inform me of the change of plan.

Okay, so it shouldn't have been the end of the world. The caregiver had given them an early lunch before she departed for the wedding and put the leftovers on separate plates in the fridge for heating up later should they still be hungry. She also advised my father of this as he was far more "together" than Shirley, despite being that much older. In fact there was no reason whatsoever for Shirley to venture into the kitchen at all.

Shirley, however, despite having been the recipient of several pep talks by many concerned parties regarding how she had to be extra careful to ensure no more falls, chose not to heed this advice.

Being fastidious by nature, she decided, unbeknown to my father, to inspect the kitchen, following the caregiver's departure, in search of possible fallen crumbs and the like. On finding what she was looking for she decided to restore the kitchen floor to its pre-lunch sparkle and thereby caused what turned out to be her worst fall ever. With one hand on her walker and wielding a mop with the other, she crashed to the floor. And re-broke a very fragile wrist that had been broken many times before.

* * *

My initial fury followed by my extreme annoyance with Shirley, due to her total disregard for her well-being by choosing to clean a floor balanced on a walker, dominated my thoughts following this her most spectacular fall. These feelings continued to be top of mind right up until such time as my "Awakening" opened me up to realising that I'd spent most of my life being furious, upset and annoyed with her – without dwelling on what had moulded her into the person she was. The thought itself was a revelation but allowing myself to understand her formative years was something else that changed my life for the better. Forever.

If we can take the time to care about and understand where others are coming from, it can help us to forgive them for what we consider to be their strange behaviour towards themselves and towards others, like ourselves. In so doing we can make our own journey on Planet Earth more comfortable to travel and as a result our lessons that much easier to learn.

* * *

'Hurry up Shirley, if we don't leave right this minute we'll miss the next bus and arrive at the cemetery far later than intended.' My highly agitated Nana, dressed from head to toe in mourner's black, held the front door open for a very dejected little Shirley. Shirley slowly placed one foot in front of the other as she reluctantly approached the door and eventually walked outside.

'Why are we … are we going there … again?' She looked up at my Nana in an imploring manner in the hope that her question, asked many times before, would at last be answered in a way she could better understand.

'How many times must I tell you Shirley,' replied my deeply emotionally stressed grandmother. 'We're going to visit Aylsa, of course, and if we're late again she'll be very sad and … and unhappy with us.' My Nana's voice almost broke with emotion and perfectly mirrored the sympathy it felt for the pain that surrounded her broken heart.

'But … I don't like visiting her there.' She'd been told many times over but Shirley, now aged four, still couldn't understand why her sister Aylsa had, at the tender age of eight, left them to go and live with someone called Jesus in a cold and dark place called a cemetery. She also couldn't understand why Jesus himself, who'd been portrayed to her as a very special and beautiful being who looked after children and grown-ups too, would have chosen to live in such a "not nice" place.

They had begun their daily walk to the bus stop, my Nana setting a brisk pace as usual, while Shirley characteristically lagged behind.

My Nana suddenly stopped and called out to her. 'Shirley, it saddens me deeply that you show such reluctance to visit Aylsa's grave … when … when it's just something we simply have to do … and something you have to get used to doing. After all, how would you feel if I buried you at a cemetery and never visited you?'

Shirley's eyes widened in fear as she shook her head to indicate she wouldn't like it at all. She also quickened her pace to catch up with her mother. 'I … I liked it better when Aylsa lived at home with us and … and I could see her all the time.'

Before replying my Nana dabbed at her already wet eyes with the handkerchief she now always carried in one hand, while taking Shirley's hand with the other, in order to cross the road to the bus stop on the other side. 'We all did Shirley, we all did.'

* * *

My mother's sister Aylsa, who was considered a very gifted child by all who knew her, had died of causes unknown at the tender age of just eight years old. Her passing occurred while six highly qualified specialists argued about the nature of her condition, which they found hard to fathom, what had caused it and what to do about it.

Shirley was just three at the time of Aylsa's untimely death and spent a year or more visiting her grave almost every weekday with my Nana. As well as on weekends when her father increased the number of mourners to three. This was not, by any stretch of the imagination, the ideal environment for a child to grow up in. My Nana spent most of her time at Aylsa's gravesite, crying, while little Shirley spent her time playing amongst the tomb stones. After a while she even brought her dolls along for companionship and to show them where Aylsa was now living.

Fortunately for Shirley, well in some respects anyway, the daily pilgrimages to Aylsa's grave grew less as time went by. They were replaced, unfortunately, by something that proved to be far more alarming. This was courtesy of my grandparents' introduction to a type of spiritualist church. The main attraction of the church heralded yet another chapter in Aylsa's life after death on Planet Earth as weekly night-time séances became a regular occurrence at Shirley's family home. They were, of course, designed to contact the dead, with special emphasis being placed, in the case of my grandparents, on being able to reach out to and communicate with Aylsa.

It also came about that many other mourners from the congregation joined my grandparents a few times a week to participate in these irregular rituals– not those officially conducted by the church itself – to ensure that their collective dead would not be able to leave this world without a fight.

It later turned out, however, that the spirits they were hooking up with were not the ones they were hoping to contact. They were in fact what is termed "earthbound spirits". Those spirits who didn't quite make it back to where they came from, due to a variety of reasons. Reasons that include fear of leaving this planet and the taking of their own lives. In other words, the spirits these weekly gatherings attracted, trapped as they were in their Neverland of anguish, were simply impersonating Aylsa and the rest of the dead. This was to establish some connection with the living mourners.

The type of unwanted spirit behaviour I have described has apparently been experienced by many people hell-bent on re-connecting with the dead through this channel of communication. But it was something unknown to my desperate grandparents until it happened.

Like all bad things, the séances didn't last, of course. Thank goodness. The group of mourners gradually became dissatisfied with the answers they were being given to pertinent questions asked of whom they at first thought to be their beloved departed. As a result the earthbound spirits sensing the frustration of the mourners, while fearing their new-found relationship with them was beginning to disintegrate, started behaving in a variety of strange and frightening ways. This all took place under the very noses of my startled grandparents and my pre-school mother.

It has also been recorded through the annals of time, by friends and members of the family, that the earthbound spirits attempted to completely take over my grandparents' home. "Things" like ornaments would fly off their resting places as would crockery and cutlery off tables while doors would open, close, slam and bedclothes would be pulled off beds and their occupants in the middle of the night.

What had started as a promising opportunity at reconnection with sorely missed loved ones turned into an untenable ordeal that only came to an end with the sale of the house. My mother, however, being just a small child at the time and as such never actually participating in the séances, claimed to have visitations from earthbound spirits from time to time throughout her life – regardless of where she was living. The most startling aspects of these visitations was the sensation of someone sitting on and pressing down on her mattress while breathing heavily into her face. These "happenings" were considered "bad nightmares" by many people she shared them with but were very real to Shirley.

I believe in retrospect that they were simply part of the ultra-challenging life she had chosen to experience this time round on Planet Earth and from which she hoped to learn corresponding lessons. It was unfortunate, therefore, that she never did seem to learn a great deal from all her experiences. Then again, neither did I learn from mine until my late awakening. On reflection it also doesn't seem as though I decided to take on as many lessons as Shirley did. But of course my life is not yet over so it's difficult to make true comparisons at this stage. With the knowledge I have learned, however, following my "Awakening" I am now better equipped than Shirley ever was to handle any adversity that this life may still present me with. And through that knowledge transform any negativity into positivity for myself.

* * *

Following the unhappy incidents surrounding the disappointing nature of the séances and the subsequent sale of their home, my grandparents cut their ties with the church and their fellow congregants – and thereby with their previously dogged desire to reunite with their beloved Aylsa. Finally and not before time, her soul was allowed to rest in peace. They did, however, continue to maintain, until their respective deaths many years apart, that she was an exceptionally gifted child whose early death could have been prevented with the right medical treatment. I, however, believe that she was here on Planet Earth for just as long as she wanted to be so as to complete what she came to achieve.

If the stories relating to Aylsa's short life were anything to go by, her parents' shared belief in her giftedness doesn't appear to be without merit. The recollections of a life well spent that ended at eight years of age also highlight that we all come to experience different facets of growth or stagnation during our lifetimes on this planet. Some souls, as in the case of Aylsa, are only here for a short while in order to complete a previous visit or visits by sharing the knowledge they acquired through lessons previously learnt. There are also others of course who need to return a multitude of times before they can eventually learn how to experience the eternally beautiful life of the eternally beautiful on Planet Earth. And there are those who are visiting for the first time and who may or may not return.

* * *

Aylsa was buried at Stellawood Cemetery next to my great grandmother who died at the ripe old age of 90. It was considered an amazing age for the times but what was even more miraculous is that she lived 82 years longer than her granddaughter.

* * *

It was supposed to be an intimate family funeral but it didn't turn out quite like that. By all accounts the procession of cars leading up the hill to the family plot seemed endless. At first my Nana had thought another funeral must have been scheduled on the same day for the next door plot. It turned out however that every occupant of every car was there to pay their respects to just one person – to Aylsa – even though most of these people were unknown to my family.

The explanation for the high turnout was revealed during discussions at the tea following the burial, and further substantiated by Aylsa's nanny.

The nanny, on the instructions of my grandmother, was in the habit of taking Aylsa to play for a few hours every day in a park close by. The first time they went there, however, the nanny was left feeling decidedly perplexed and more than a little afraid. While watching Aylsa happily swaying to and fro on one of the swings she nodded off for a while in the soothing autumn sunshine. When she woke up Aylsa was nowhere to be seen. She panicked at first and looked for her everywhere but without success. She was in fact on the verge of running back to the house and confessing her sleep-ridden crime to my Nana, of having lost her charge, when Aylsa suddenly re-appeared. She had been wreathed in smiles and gave her nanny a warm hug by way of apology for her disappearance.

Every day thereafter the same thing would happen. The nanny would take the opportunity to catch a little snooze in the sun while Aylsa disappeared for a couple of hours. Yet as she always returned in good time to go home, the nanny chose to overlook her absences. When quizzed after the funeral, the shame-faced nanny admitted that she had been concerned about Aylsa's disappearance on day one but thereafter it became the norm and as Aylsa always came back in good health and spirits she assumed she shouldn't worry. More importantly, she was also concerned that if she told my Nana about these disappearances, she might get Aylsa into trouble.

So what was Aylsa actually doing during these daily absences from the park? Well I have already mentioned that she was an unusually gifted child but even I was sceptical the first time her escapades were described to me. As so many family friends and members attested to their validity, however, I have come to the conclusion that the claims must be rooted in truth.

As the story goes Aylsa was in fact spending her time visiting people who lived in and around the neighbourhood but only those who were ill or suffering in one form or the other. These were the same people who attended her funeral and who all testified as to what an incredibly wonderful little person she was and how she had positively touched each and every one of their lives. This was reported as they all fell over themselves with gratitude when describing their individual relationships with her.

'I must congratulate you on a wonderful little daughter, May, Aylsa was a very special child who brought a great deal of joy into my life through her visits.'

'Goodness, so she visited you too? How extraordinary,' commented another. 'For our part we just can't believe she's gone – we began to feel she had replaced our little girl who was stillborn and who we mourned terribly.'

'I was recovering from surgery when I first met her. I thought I'd never recover to tell you the truth. But Aylsa changed my mind about that. A few visits from her and well … I felt a new calm in my life … until I received the untimely news of her death, of course …'

'I first encountered Aylsa on a day I was sitting in my garden crying loudly with anguish at the loss of my mother who'd died just a few days prior. Aylsa simply popped her pretty little head over the hedge and asked if she could come in and sit with me for a while. What a remarkable child.'

'She was like a little angel.'

'She certainly was. It was hard to think that the words of wisdom she spoke came out of the mouth of one so young.'

'Indeed. My sentiments entirely.'

'Yes, an angel, that's a very good description of her. It seemed to me that God had suddenly blessed me with her presence because up until then I wasn't sure how I was going to cope without my dear wife. Aylsa's beautiful angelic smile was enough to transform my darkest days into ones of hope.'

'It's going to be hard to imagine life without her.'

'I agree. It's not going to be easy to live without her visits.'

'I know what you mean – in reality I knew her for such a short time but it seemed as though I'd known her forever.'

The comments and accolades regarding Aylsa continued throughout the afternoon.

My aunt Edith, Nana's sister, also contributed her special remembrance of Aylsa … 'You know my dear,' she remarked to one of the mourners, 'I was reminded, when you mentioned earlier how Aylsa had helped you over the untimely death of your sister … just how much she helped us in a similar situation. Our baby sister Elizabeth, who we called Lizzie, also died young, a few months prior to Aylsa's seventh birthday in fact and it's hard to believe the child's wisdom even then. 'Don't cry,' she said to me at the time, 'Lizzie is now with God. He usually takes full blown flowers to be with him in heaven but sometimes he just swoops down and picks a little bud.'

'Oh my goodness,' exclaimed the woman Edith was speaking with, who almost dropped her teacup in the process, 'she could have been describing her own forthcoming death.'

'Well, yes,' nodded Edith in agreement while dabbing at her eyes with a serviette … but Aylsa did have psychic powers you know, of that we were all convinced. Do tell them about the incident of the broken doll, Maysie,' she said to my Nana who was walking by handing out fresh cups of tea. Taking the opportunity of sitting down for a while my Nana began sharing her contribution to the many talents of her dearly departed and sorely missed little Aylsa.

'It was just a couple of weeks ago … she'd only been in hospital a few days but was very ill ... my poor darling.' Nana had to compose herself before continuing. Edith gently patted her shoulder to give her encouragement and she eventually continued. 'I had bent over her in her hospital bed to apply a damp face cloth to her forehead in order to cool her fevered brow when she whispered in my ear, "Don't be cross with Shirley, Mummy." I was obviously a bit taken aback by her comment.

"Why would I be cross with her darling?"

"She … she had a little accident – she broke her Margaret doll."

"Oh ... oh really," I replied, "but darling, I picked Margaret up off the floor in the playroom this morning and put her on a chair – she seemed fine."

Aylsa continued as if I hadn't said a word. "And she's hidden her behind the doll's house … because she doesn't want you to know … she's afraid you'll be angry with her."

'I thought she might be slightly delirious due to the strong medications the doctors were administering to her so I kissed her and reassured her that I wouldn't be cross with Shirley. But when I returned home from the hospital much later that day, I was strangely drawn to the playroom to check on the doll Aylsa had referred to.

I found Margaret with her permanently smiling face totally at odds with the hole in her head and one badly broken arm dangling from her side. She was squashed between the wall and the doll's house just where Aylsa had said she could be found.'

My Nana politely allowed for a number of gasps and murmurings from the mourners listening to the story before continuing.

'Normally I would have immediately discussed the matter of the broken doll with Shirley in order to reassure her that accidents happen and that she should never be afraid to tell me anything. Somehow, though, a broken doll seemed unimportant when compared to how broken she herself was when Aylsa first fell ill and went to hospital. Not to mention her reaction when I told her that the angels had come for Aylsa and taken her away to live with Jesus.

Shirley has cried every day since the death of her sister and wanders around the house calling her name. It's as if she doesn't quite believe she's no longer here. And to be honest neither do I.'

* * *

Something else that happened, many years later, but which interestingly enough fits very well within the context of Aylsa's life and death on Planet Earth, concerns me.

Although, as previously mentioned, my Nana eventually gave up on reconnecting with her dearest Aylsa during this lifetime, she never totally got over her untimely death and prayed constantly to be re-united with her in a future life. With the advent of my arrival, however, her faith in realising this desire appeared to have been prematurely achieved.

By all accounts she announced, shortly after my birth, to all and sundry and with unbridled joy that God had answered her prayers sooner than she imagined would be the case. She believed Aylsa had in fact been returned to her in this lifetime in the form of yours truly.

This no doubt explains my Nana's enduring love for and devotion to me, even though, I must hasten to add, I have sadly never been able to demonstrate any of the gifts that Aysla possessed. A similar physical resemblance is the only thing from my perspective that we appear to share.

This belief of Nana's that Aylsa was returned to her in my form does however give greater meaning to our special bond and why Nana's untimely death when I was just twelve years old made me initially feel that life without her wasn't going to be worth living.

It was no doubt the same anguish that Nana herself had felt at the loss of Aylsa.

# Chapter 20

# Signing my Mother's Death Warrant

Shirley suffered a terrible death. The memory of it haunted me for ages. But only when I allowed myself to think about it.

* * *

'I have to insist you give your permission and that you give it immediately. Your mother has to be operated on without delay.'

The surgeon I introduced you to in a previous chapter extended the release form, neatly clipped to a board, in my direction. His pen lay precariously balanced on top of it but somehow it managed to make its slow motion journey from his hands to mine without falling from the clipboard to the floor. It seemed at the time as though everything was moving in a sort of unreal slow motion despite being underpinned by the urgent reality of the situation.

We were standing at my mother's bedside in the ward hastily allocated to her on our arrival at the hospital, following her latest, and as it turned out, her last fall. The one brought about by the cleaning of the kitchen floor on her caregiver's unscheduled day off.

'Don't you dare do anything of the sort Ingrid. How very, very rude of the two of you to stand here and discuss my fate in a manner that suggests you don't even consider me to be present …'

'You leave me with no other option as you yourself have refused to co-operate …' The surgeon's voice trailed off as Shirley, ignoring his interjection, continued her tirade. 'I didn't have to have an operation with the last break … you told me yourself that bandaging the broken bones together was a far safer option than operating on me at this stage of my life … so why do you want to persecute me now?

The medical profession killed my mother,' she screamed, 'and now you want to kill me.' From enraged dragon slayer intent on a kill if she wasn't obeyed, Shirley disintegrated into helpless crying child mode, as only she could do. 'Even when I'm not well all you want to do is be nasty to me.'

Shirley sobbed uncontrollably. One of the nurses gently massaged her frail shoulders while I stood rooted to the spot, frozen in time, the dreaded pen clasped in my clammy hand, demanding my signature.

Although Shirley's comments were chiefly aimed at me it was the surgeon who, reading the extreme anxiety on my face, stepped in to try and make an attempt to pacify her. Yet in his customary manner his words came across as less than reassuring. 'I'm sorry you feel like that. I simply want what's best for you. This is a *far worse* fracture than the one you experienced the last time you broke this wrist.' He turned his attention away from Shirley and once more concentrated his urgent gaze on me. 'You've seen the x-rays with your own eyes,' he implored, 'this time the bones are exposed and if we don't operate soon we risk an infection that could turn nasty.'

So Shirley's operation came to pass against her will and to all intents and purpose like a death sentence imposed on her by the stroke of a pen – administered by the hand of her own horrid, unloving and uncaring daughter.

* * *

'I've just been to the hospital to see your mother and she's looking far from well. I think you should get yourself over there as soon as possible.' These alarming words were conveyed to me via my cell phone, and to my surprise, by my soon to be ex-husband. I knew by the fact that he'd phoned me in the first place, and by the tone of his voice that things were definitely serious.

Despite her frailty Shirley had by all accounts sailed through this operation just as she had done during so many previous procedures. But this time, unfortunately, she never got to drop anchor in calm waters.

When I had phoned the hospital following her surgery earlier that morning I was advised not to visit her until the afternoon. Although she'd come through her surgery without complications she needed to rest. So to get his call just a few hours later was worrying in the extreme. My heart started to beat just a little bit faster as I closed down my computer and hurriedly prepared to leave. I drove as fast as I could and arrived at the hospital in record time but was definitely not prepared for the grim sight that met me.

A very pale and wan Shirley was already in ICU. A long tube inserted into her airways protruded from her mouth while her slim little wrists were tied to the iron armrests of her hospital bed. I was horror stricken and once again experienced the same helplessness as I had felt when I was beseeched to provide my permission for her procedure.

'But why have you tied her arms down like that,' I exclaimed, close to tears, 'she's not likely to try and run away. Does she look as though she's got any strength to do that?' It was then explained to me that it was a measure that had to be taken to prevent her trying to pull the ventilator tube out of her throat. It was something she had in fact already attempted. Although she'd come through her surgery in a very satisfactory condition a few hours earlier, she'd suddenly developed flu that had just as quickly turned to pneumonia.

'But why does she have to have that ghastly ventilator thing shoved down her throat anyway, you can see how distressed it's making her? It can't be helpful surely?' The gurgling sounds coming from the revolting contraption confirmed what I was saying. The sister in charge was quick to reply but I always felt that what she conveyed to me was said more in an attempt to placate me rather than to share the true state of Shirley's condition. 'We may be able to take her off the ventilator … if … if the meds prescribed do what they're intended to do … but for the moment she can't breathe without it.'

The worst thing about the whole ordeal was the combined look of terror, hatred and helplessness that shone from Shirley's eyes. Her eyes were one of her most expressive features so I didn't need to be told what the looks I was receiving meant.

'Ingrid how dare you let them do this to me? Get this tube out of me immediately. Don't you have any compassion for me at all? What have I done to deserve a daughter like you? I begged you not to give your consent to this operation but no, you always think you know what's best, don't you? Why, oh why, couldn't you just listen to me for once in your life?' Although none of these words actually fell from her lips due to the ventilator preventing speech, they definitely fell from her eyes.

I was so shocked at her condition and imploring looks that I was unable to talk to her at first. Once I'd managed to acknowledge to myself that she had been right and that I should never have agreed to her procedure courtesy of my signature, I started to try and explain my actions while fighting back my tears of remorse.

'I'm so sorry Mum, you were right, I shouldn't have given my consent, I … I just … well the surgeon said it was for the best and that … that I had no option and I thought I didn't but … but I didn't know that you were going to develop flu and breathing problems that … that have necessitated this ventilator.' The word pneumonia was one I couldn't bring myself to utter. I kept it to myself even though I was almost sure she would have heard one of the nurses refer to it. 'But you will recover Mum I know you will.' I tried to sound more convinced of this than I felt. 'After all … *I'm* the one in the family with breathing problems … not you'.

I had tried to make a pathetic attempt at levity in the overbearingly heavy situation in which I found myself but needless to say the expression in her eyes never faltered for an instant. It also refused to alter even when I said something that I'd never told her before in my entire life.

'I love you Mum.' There seemed to be a lump of acid in my throat which was holding back my tears and making my statement barely audible.

To be truthful all I wanted to do was run away. I knew my tears were about to flow and perhaps that would upset her even more than my unhelpful presence. She wasn't, after all, used to me blubbing all over her. She probably wouldn't like it very much either.

A nurse, carrying a tray of needles, came to my rescue. She whispered that Shirley was ready for more sedation. She also informed me that the ward doctor had arrived and wished to speak with me in the passage regarding the need for the ventilator.

* * *

The next alarming phone call regarding Shirley's post-operative condition came from the hospital early the following morning. After unsuccessfully trying my cell phone, which I'd switched off out of habit before succumbing to the welcome effect of a sleeping pill, they tried my landline. It was the loud and persistent shrill of that instrument next to my bed that eventually cut through my medically induced slumber. 'Your mother has taken a turn for the worse, we think you should come through to the hospital as soon as you can.'

It was a nameless, faceless person on the other end of the line but she immediately had my attention. 'I … I'll come straight away, I gulped.' I was suddenly wide awake.

When I got to the hospital I was told she had passed away. I later found out from the friend who'd kindly driven me there, to help alleviate some of the pressure I was under, that hospitals are apparently well known for phoning and telling people their loved one has taken a bad turn – and asking them to come to the hospital soonest. When you arrive they inform you that the patient has passed on. What they don't tell you is that the death occurred before they even made the call.

I was strangely grateful for that. *Imagine,* I thought, *the added trauma of driving to the hospital knowing that you were already too late to say your goodbyes.*

* * *

As we leave this mortal coil our whole life is supposed to flash before our eyes. I have often wondered what flashed before Shirley's eyes and whether the following could possibly do her experience any justice?

*The start of her new life on Planet Earth via a relatively stress-free birth.*

*The love showered on her, the baby of the family, by all members of it.*

*The special love she received from her sister Aylsa, five years her senior.*

*Tabby, the sweet little family cat she was always trying to pick up but which continually managed to escape her clutches.*

*All the wonderful toys in the playroom.*

*Playing with Aylsa.*

*The death of Aylsa.*

*The loss of her parents too as they busied themselves trying to reconnect with the deceased Aylsa and in so doing almost forgot she existed.*

*The monotonous day after day playtime routine at the deeply depressing cemetery when visiting Aylsa.*

*The frightening séances, a continuing feature of weekly life at her family home.*

*The equally frightening visitations by earthbound spirits that marred her pre-school years. And continued to haunt her throughout her existence.*

*The return of her parents to her life following the sale of their spirit-invaded home and the abandonment of their obsession at re-connecting with Aylsa.*

*The return of her mother's joy for life and entertaining having come to accept Aylsa's passing at long last.*

*Her exceptional gifts for playing the piano and singing first identified at school by her music teacher.*

*Practicing and practicing.*

*The death of her beloved father.*

*Her short-lived glory as a fledgling concert pianist.*

*Her burning desire to concentrate her talents on developing her soprano voice in order to become an accomplished opera singer.*

*Practicing and practicing her scales with total dedication.*

*The encouragement she received from her mother.*

*Practicing her scales and practicing her scales.*

*Discovering that achieving her goal to become an opera singer of note wasn't going to prove as easy as she had hoped.*

*A few unhappy relationships.*

*A cancelled engagement while continuing with her desire to achieve success in the limited world of opera that existed in South Africa at the time.*

*Her approval of her mother's remarriage to a family friend.*

*Her mother's disapproval of most of her relationships but her continued support for Shirley's singing aspirations.*

*Eventually meeting Bill, some years her senior, and someone her mother totally approved of.*

*Her decision to marry Bill while still hoping to advance her singing career from within the marriage.*

*The wedding.*

*The honeymoon.*

*Her unplanned pregnancy with her only child.*

*The pain and suffering the birth caused her.*

*Migraine headaches that started shortly after the birth and continued throughout most of her life.*

*Her final realisation that her singing career was over.*

*Her unhappy relationship with her daughter during the childhood years.*

*Her attempted suicide following the death of her mother.*

*The discovery that she had developed cancer of the womb.*

*Her hysterectomy.*

*Her frightening and violently ill-making cancer treatments.*

*The unhappy relationship with her daughter that continued into early adulthood and beyond.*

*The short-lived joy her daughter's engagement to a UK journalist provided.*

*The deep disappointment when her daughter cancelled the wedding.*

*The continuation of the unhappy relationship with her daughter.*

*Her disappointment that her daughter initially chose to remain overseas instead of returning and carving out a meaningful life back in South Africa.*

*Her restored joy when her daughter did eventually return, meet and marry someone she totally approved of.*

*Her ongoing joy at what she perceived to be the perfect married life they were leading.*

*Her utter despair when they divorced.*

*Her ongoing ill-health.*

*The many falls and breaks her osteoporotic bones endured.*

*The many operations she endured.*

*Her misery at being removed from her home and being installed in a retirement village at the insistence of her daughter.*

*Her ongoing misery at living in the retirement village.*

*The claustrophobic environment of her home in the retirement village that caused much unhappiness in her relationship with her husband.*

*Her disgust at being asked to play old music hall favourites like 'Daisy Daisy' for the occupants of the retirement village once the entertainment committee discovered she played the piano. And her refusal to do so.*

*Her unhappiness that her daughter didn't visit her more often. Did her daughter think arriving with groceries and gifts made up for her sporadic visits?*

*Her happiness at the visits of her son-in-law before and after the divorce.*

*Her unhappiness that her hearing was becoming impaired but her refusal to wear her hearing aid because quite simply it ruined her hairstyle. What was worse, she wondered, being able to hear but being seen with one's hair looking a total mess?*

*The day-to-day monotony of living in a closed environment shared with her caregiver and her husband.*

*The once a week visit by her selfish daughter who chose to busy herself with running a business rather than visiting her parents daily.*

*The dreadful food prepared by the caregiver and the mess she made in the kitchen.*

*The cleaning of the kitchen floor.*

*The fall.*

*The break.*

*The insistence of the surgeon and her selfish daughter that she undergo surgery.*

*The operation.*

*The relief at surviving the operation despite not feeling that well following it.*

*The joy of being visited by her son-in-law.*

*The despair of falling asleep after his visit and waking up with an uncomfortable ventilator tube placed down her throat that rendered her incapable of speaking.*

*The double despair of trying to remove the tube and being rewarded by the indignity and discomfort of having her arms tied to her hospital bed.*

*The anger at and resentment of her selfish daughter who had given her consent for the operation and for what was now happening to her.*

*At last the arrival of her daughter to assist her in removing the frightening tube from her body.*

*Her utter amazement when her daughter did nothing to assist her in this regard.*

*The crocodile tears shed by her daughter who had mumbled something about loving her. How could a person love another and treat them so badly?*

*More sedation.*

*More sleep.*

*Waking up again to discover the dreaded tube still in place.*

*The ongoing discomfort.*

*The absence of  her daughter at her bedside.*

*She understood that it was too difficult for her frail husband to visit her but where was Ingrid?*

*Abandoned.*

*Sore back.*

*Difficulty in breathing.*

*Gasping and gurgling.*

*Holding on to this life with difficulty.*

*Peace at last.*

*No more pain. No more suffering.*

# Chapter 21

# Forgiving Shirley for Everything She Didn't do to Me

Her death left me more devastated than I could have ever imagined.

The stark realisation that she had departed my life and would never return was not in the least bit easy to come to terms with. I suddenly felt there were things we still needed to discuss. So much left unsaid. Her death was after all extremely sudden following what was initially considered to be a good recovery from her procedure.

The guilt of course left a worrisome legacy. Why, I kept asking myself, had I been in such a hurry to give my consent to her operation, despite the pressure that was brought to bear by the surgeon.

So what if she'd developed an infection and died as a result of it. At least she wouldn't have developed pneumonia and suffered the indignity and horror of having to endure that awful ventilator tube being thrust down her throat.

I could see with my own eyes that it had been extremely uncomfortable for her but had it been very painful too? The ward doctor reassured me that it wouldn't have been painful but how would he have known – he'd never had one shoved down his throat had he? 'No,' he had admitted, he had not. 'But provided ventilator tubes are inserted correctly there is no pain involved,' he had said. I had hoped like hell that Shirley's had been inserted correctly and made a note to have a "Living Will" drawn up excluding any ventilator tubes from being inserted in my throat for any futuristic reason.

Everyone continued to reassure me over and over again in the days that followed her death that I really hadn't had a choice in the matter – I had been more or less forced to give my consent. Their reassurances, however, although well intended, were totally unable to remove the acute and stubborn feelings of blameworthiness that haunted me.

Even as I prepared for her memorial service, I was unable to shake my new worst enemies and constant companions, "remorse and guilt", from sitting down with me at my computer as I composed her eulogy the night before.

I decided that in view of our awkward relationship, sloppy sentimental words would be inappropriate and to concentrate more on her talents and pre-marital accomplishments instead.

I typed up quite a few drafts before settling on one I thought covered Shirley's life in a meaningful way. I then printed out a copy and carried it through to my bedroom to have a final re-read in bed and make corrections if necessary.

I also decided to forego my usual shower in favour of a comforting hot bath before getting into bed. Writing the eulogy had drained me more than I thought it would as it reminded me once more that Shirley was no longer going to be part of my life. It also highlighted for me, on reflection, how most of her life had been marred with sadness and in some instances with regret too – although I did not allow those observations to taint what I had written.

People attending memorial services are already in sad mode anyway, why make the experience worse, I asked myself. I therefore decided to steer away altogether from any unhappy extracts from her life and make her eulogy as happy and amusing as possible. So that people giving up their afternoon soap operas at the retirement village would still feel entertained.

As I busied myself with running my bath and adding a soothing herbal tonic to the water, I was surprised to hear the door to my bedroom slam. When I went to investigate, I found it firmly shut. My first thought was that I must have left the French Doors leading onto the outside balcony open but when I went to check I found them not only shut but locked. Wondering if I had left any other outside doors open around the house that could in turn have caused a draft and the subsequent slamming of the door, I went to check on all of them but I drew blanks all round.

In so doing I was also further reminded that it was a calm night devoid of wind. Puzzled by what could have caused the door to slam I climbed into bed following my superficially soothing bath and proceeded to read through Shirley's eulogy again.

It was with deep sadness that I eventually switched off my bedside light, and uncharacteristically for me, cried myself to sleep. Once more I had found myself thinking about the sad and unhappy aspects of her life – those I hadn't included in the eulogy.

I also realised for the first time that I had come into this world gasping for air and that she had left it gasping for the same thing. I found the correlation both troubling and profound.

* * *

I'm not sure at what point during my troubled sleep that it happened. I was gently awakened however by the feeling of being firmly yet lovingly held, in slender arms that seemed to possess abnormally great strength as they drew me along the mattress to the centre of my bed. I would normally have been terrified by such an experience but in this instance I felt inexplicably safe. Unfortunately, although I have relived the happening in my mind many times over, I must admit that I still don't have the words to do justice to what transpired that night. All I can say is that it felt as though I was being drawn into a warm embrace of reassurance specially designed to absolve me of all my adverse feelings of responsibility for my mother's death.

Even though I had been told repeatedly over the years about the séances and visitations that had occurred at my grandparents' home during my mother's early childhood, I had more often than not taken what was said with a pinch of salt. I came to realise, however, that this encounter, coupled with the strange phenomenon of the slamming door, was designed to leave me in no doubt. Shirley had paid me a visit before finally departing this lifetime, as she had "things" to convey to me that she wasn't able to do while she lived on Planet Earth.

* * *

In my unenlightened state back then though, I wasn't able to see all the dimensions and ramifications of her visit. As far as I was concerned Shirley had visited me for one reason only, to forgive me for causing her very unhappy end – and I had been extremely grateful for that, then.

It was only after my "Awakening" that I was able to comprehend the rest and what a wonderful experience that proved to be.

I not only came to understand that her physical death freed her up to affectionately demonstrate her great love for me, during her deeply comforting visit, in a way she could never bring herself to do during our pre-ordained lives together. I also came to understand that Shirley had not dropped in on me that night to forgive me because there was nothing to forgive. She came to reassure me that she had brought the circumstances of her demise upon herself without the help of anyone else.

Through that knowledge I have also come to *further* understand that just like Shirley we are all responsible for everything that happens to us. The good and the bad experiences are all of our own making from the time we enter this lifetime until we depart. No matter how difficult or rewarding our path may turn out to be what transpires during it can never be the responsibility of someone else.

As a result of my newly enlightened state, I have also been able to forgive Shirley for all the adverse stuff I previously accused her of but that she *didn't* do to me during our interwoven lives.

I had after all selected her to be my mother and to learn everything I wanted her to teach me. She on the other hand chose me to be her daughter so that she could receive the lessons she knew I would be able to provide.

Once I'd been able to recognise the roles both of us had played in the other's life, the knowledge also allowed me to see the many difficulties Shirley decided to endure in order to grow. Sadly though, they were difficulties she was mostly unable to overcome during this lifetime she shared with me.

It has also given me the opportunity to thank her by way of prayer and meditation for everything that she has done for me. I have been so very fortunate to learn and grow from the times that we shared.

Love you Mum. Love you always. I am eternally blessed and eternally grateful to have had you as a mother.

# Epilogue

I have made many mentions of my "Awakening" and my subsequent "Enlightenment" throughout this book. This may in turn have set up a question mark with you as regards how my "Awakening" came about and why I haven't explained the circumstances of it.

The reason is that as my book unfolded in the way it was meant to, and at a pace it was meant to, I knew that the right spot to convey this information to you would present itself. I was also aware that it couldn't be inserted into any one particular chapter as it had a place in all of them.

I am, however, happy to report that this space has revealed itself to be the right one. After all nothing can be forced or rushed. There is always a right time and place for everything. So it was with my Awakening too.

I hope I'm not going to disappoint you when I say that it wasn't the amazing spectacle that every person I have previously shared it with expected me to describe. There was no trumpeting of angels, flashes of blinding awareness or my Maker floating in on a cloud to welcome me back to the fold. Nothing like that at all. Instead my Awakening simply and gently came about at a time in my life when I was ready to receive it.

Looking back along my path to enlightenment I recognise that it only started in a meaningful way much later in my chronological life than I would have liked.

Initially, I had only been exposed to the religious beliefs of a wide variety of faiths all seemingly fighting with one another to be "the answer". None of these individual beliefs resonated with me one hundred per cent however – in fact as time went by just the opposite occurred. I began to dislike religion and its followers, who I facetiously dubbed the God squad, so much that I'm ashamed to say I set about arming myself with knowledge that I could use to put it and them down.

I certainly didn't believe in God, I decided, and as a result I didn't believe in myself – although I didn't know at the time that the two beliefs are synonymous. My favourite joke in fact that my friends always encouraged me to repeat at social gatherings bears testament to my then point of view. 'Tell us again Ingrid, what are the two things you fear most in life,' they would chorus. I would reply without hesitation. 'Becoming a bored northern suburbs housewife and a reborn Christian.' This always produced gales of laughter, the loudest contributor being me.

My interest in the purely spiritual realm wasn't that strong in the beginning either. It was an interest simply born out of curiosity but fortunately for me it grew. I read all the spiritual books I could lay my hands on. I also attended a great number of spiritual workshops, to not only challenge their content as was my quest in life at that time but to try and find out what all the hype was about. But I never quite got it. Not until "it" finally got me.

I came home early, for me, one Friday night, after experiencing yet another seemingly empty outing filled with indistinct alcohol saturated conversation, largely obliterated by loud music. I was deeply depressed. And once more asked questions of myself and whoever else might be listening. 'What the *hell* is this existence of mine all about? Why can't I change my life into one I want to live? Why do I experience the same old, same old, over and over again? What do I have to do to be truly happy?' There was no reply as usual.

As I am a night-owl, however, it wasn't sufficiently late for me to feel tired enough to escape to bed and sleep. Instead of switching on my TV, turning to my current book or going onto my computer for diversion from my troubled self, I checked my phone and came across something that would change my life. It was a saved email with a link that had been sent to me following the attendance of a recent spiritual workshop. The first I'd attended in a long while.

In a fairly disinterested manner I laid my sad-self down on the couch, pressed the link and began to listen to the message. Although I had heard most of everything that was being conveyed a million times before in many different ways by a multitude of spiritual teachers, for some inexplicable reason it all suddenly started to make sense to me.

Don't ask me how or why or if there was anything particularly intellectual about the experience. All I can tell you is this. To use an old cliché "I began to see the light". Not a light exploding in my being like an untold number of fireworks being released into the night sky. It was instead the gentle light of my inner spirit quietly coming back to life as I began to cry a zillion tears of joy at the rekindling of a deep and exquisite feeling of love for my Maker, and as a result for myself.

I shed buckets of joy, on and off, in the weeks that followed and continue to this day to be brought to tears of equal joy every time I recall my "Awakening" that reminded me of who I truly am and why this life I am living is so precious.

I am an eternal spirit who is loved beyond belief by my Maker with whom I am "one". I am no longer alone and will never ever again experience the unreality of being alone. I am back where I belong, together with my maker, appreciating the glorious love that has always been part of me – despite experiencing a feeling of disconnection from it for so long.

Now however, having rekindled this once dormant love, I am happy and content in the knowledge that come what may it is the love that will never desert me. It will be with me forever more no matter how much of it I choose to give away to everyone else. I now also understand that the more love I give, the more love I receive as that is the way our Maker has always intended it to be. For without love there is nothing to give or receive.

As a result of finding myself again, I am also experiencing more and more of the eternally beautiful life of the eternally beautiful right here on Planet Earth. With every passing day. The same beautiful life, I am guided to believe by my inner spirit, that I have experienced with absolute joy so many times before. In the hereafter.

# Acknowledgements

When I started compiling my list of acknowledgements I soon realised just how very many wonderful souls on Planet Earth have at one time or another, over the years, contributed to my thought processes and as a result to my writing.

I also realised though, that to mention all of them would result in me having to write another book instead of a list. So I decided to confine my group of "most cherished contributors" to the circle of "now". The special friends and spiritual teachers who are with me and support me in every moment.

I have known many of them for a long time while I have come to know the others more recently. All of them, however, have one thing in common, they are all part and parcel of the way I think, live and write. Now.

Let me start with the special friends. Those who lovingly encouraged me every step of the way during the writing of my book. They did this by not only selflessly participating in the reading of it in its various stages of development but also by offering their observations and advice along the way. Some even went further in their quest to assist me by offering constructive comment on the book's cover during its development.

Kim, Caroline, Lin and Carole, I love you all and thank you all for allowing me to bring you into my life to be my dear friends, teachers and confidantes. I would also like to extend a special thank you to Eva, my dear Venice friend, who has not only lent her name to my book but has always been such a wonderful source of encouragement. I have learned so much from all of you.

Then there are the special spiritual teachers. Those who regardless of whether they are still living on Planet Earth or not, continue to have such a positive influence on me by providing up to the minute inspiration. This is not only due to their mind blowing and prolific teachings but also through their talent for sharing the important stuff in a way that has everlasting relevance, right now.

They are: Deepak Chopra, Wayne Dyer, Kahlil Gibran, Louise Hay, Jesus in a Course in Miracles, The Dalai Lama, Ashraf Moorad, Carolyn Myss, Eckhart Tolle, Marianne Williamson.

I would also like to thank Jo-Anne Richards, Richard Beynon and Melinda Ferguson from whom I have gained valuable knowledge.

And finally I would like to acknowledge my Physical Jerks Instructor who asked repeatedly to be mentioned in my book – 'Hi Jaclyn'.

---

If you'd like to share any part or parts of your life's journey with me or ask me any questions I would love to hear from you.

INGRID LOMAS
www.ingridlomas.com
hi@ingridlomas.com

www.ingramcontent.com/pod-product-compliance
Ingram Content Group UK Ltd.
Pitfield, Milton Keynes, MK11 3LW, UK
UKHW041635190726
13854UKWH00006B/2506